Cleveland CHRISTMAS Memories

LOOKING BACK AT HOLIDAYS PAST

Gail Ghetia Bellamy

GRAY & COMPANY, PUBLISHERS
CLEVELAND

To George Ghetia and Laurie Orr,
my brother and sister,
who helped create so many of my
Merry Christmas memories.

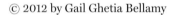

© 2012 by Gail Ghetia Bellamy

Gray & Company, Publishers
www.grayco.com

Designed by Laurence J. Nozik

ISBN: 978-1-938441-08-0

Printed in the United States of America

CONTENTS

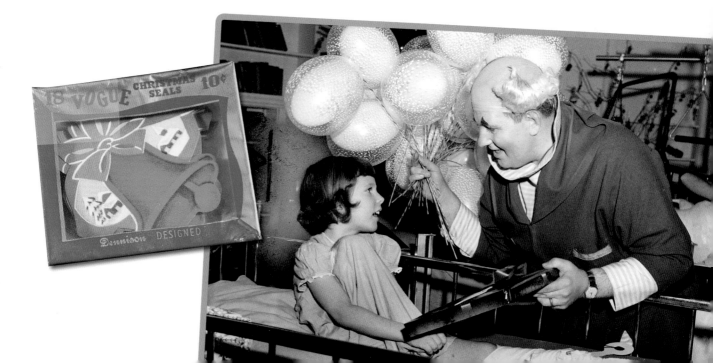

INTRODUCTION

Nostalgia is all about the things we loved and the things we miss today. In the not-too-distant past, store clerks weren't shy about wishing us a Merry Christmas and we did window shopping rather than Web surfing for gift ideas. Happy memories for Clevelanders include taking the rapid transit downtown to see the grandeur of a decorated and bustling Euclid Avenue in December. We recall the sparkle and splendor of department stores decked out for Christmas.

As kids, we made forays into the neighborhood toy stores and hobby shops to check out the gifts we wanted Santa to bring us. We embraced the magic of the vast toy departments of Cleveland's now-closed department stores, and displays in discount stores, drugstores, and dime stores. Each of us has memories of a gift we pined for as a child. Some favorites are Chatty Cathy dolls, Cabbage Patch Kids, Rock 'Em Sock 'Em Robots and Schwinn Sting-Ray Orange Krate bicycles.

At home, delicious aromas emanated from Mom's kitchen, as cookie-baking and pastry-making got underway. No sooner had we finished eating our leftover Thanksgiving turkey sandwiches on the day after Thanksgiving, than it was time to head downtown for the annual tree lighting ceremony with Santa. The Friday after Thanksgiving was also the day Mr. Jingeling's television appearances started for the Christmas season.

As the pre-Christmas excitement built, we bought Advent calendars and counted the days until Christmas. We braved the cold at Christmas parades held the Saturday after Thanksgiving. We watched as the city-wide decorations gradually unfolded downtown. Garlands went up at Higbee's, and oversized exterior ornaments appeared at the May Company. Halle's and Higbee's unveiled that year's window displays, and the Sterling-Lindner tree stood, majestic and decorated, waiting for admirers. Soon the signs were everywhere: Salvation Army bell ringers stood outside store entrances. Businesses held their annual Christmas parties.

When it came time to start our serious Christmas shopping, we withdrew money from our Christmas Club savings account at the bank, redeemed our books of trading stamps, got out our store Charge-A-Plates, and studied department store and mail-order catalogs. We left nose prints on the windows as we gazed at Christmas displays. We bought tickets for Christmas plays, ballets, and concerts. We started stuffing tips into envelopes for the milkman and others who delivered baked goods, potato chips, newspapers, and dry cleaning to our door.

We sent Christmas cards, many of them created locally at American Greetings. We were awed by the Christmas lighting displays at GE's Nela Park. At home, families put their favorite Christmas music on the hi-fi: selections such as *Bing Crosby's White Christmas* (1949), *Spike Jones Presents a Xmas Spectacular* (1956), *Christmas With the Chipmunks* (1962), *Frank Yankovic's Christmas Party* polka album (1964), and *The Jackson 5 Christmas Album* (1970)—as they decorated the tree. The whole family watched *A Christmas Story* one more time, and recited the dialogue along with the characters. Carolers went door to door.

Each family and each ethnic community had its own traditions as the season built to a crescendo with Christmas pageants, nativity scenes, and much-anticipated Christmas Eve and Christmas Day services at church. For our Christmas feasts, we brought out the once-a-year tablecloths and Christmas table settings. Perhaps we even set the table with Christmas Eve patterned dinnerware designed by Cleveland artist and industrial designer Viktor Schreckengost. The book *Cleveland Food Memories* is filled with examples of how food links us to our family and our culture. It's not surprising, then, that what we ate for Christmas dinner depended on who we were, and what our families considered traditional. Some had meatless meals, fish, pasta, or oyster stew on Christmas Eve. For Christmas Day, turkey, ham, roast beef, rabbit, pheasant, or pork were among the standards.

Collectively these memories represent wonderful Cleveland Christmases that are gone forever. We can look back, though. We can read about them, and remember the people who made them so special.

COUNTER CULTURE: Christmas shopping at Higbee's, 1965.

CHRISTMAS, CLEVELAND-STYLE

Christmas Shopping: The Downtown Pilgrimage

WHAT'S IN STORE FOR CHRISTMAS?

DEPARTMENT STORE MEMORIES

Excursions to downtown Cleveland were rich with Christmas experiences. Cleveland kids recall taking in the animated displays in department store windows, paying visits to Santa and Mr. Jingeling, and experiencing the splendor of the stores along Euclid Avenue. While the major attractions were Higbee's, May Company, Halle's, and Sterling-Lindner, Clevelanders also remember stopping at drug stores, dime stores, restaurants, cafeterias, and riding the rapid transit.

HIGBEE'S

Higbee's at Christmas was almost as much a Cleveland landmark as the Terminal Tower itself. Christmas was in the air on Public Square, and the sensory bombardment of Higbee's was a major contributor. Everything from the window displays to the lavish first-floor decorations to finding lunch in a little stove on dollhouse-sized dishes at Higbee's Silver Grille added to the allure. Kids had a chance to shop solo for their parents after passing through the small entranceway at The Twigbee Shop, and of course Santa was waiting to see them, too. Higbee's is definitely a part of the fond memories Cleveland's kids built around Christmas.

FUN IN THE OVEN:
Higbee's Silver Grille stove, from which the much-beloved children's lunch was served.

Joe Valenti, who today operates Flower Child, a retro vintage shop and museum on Cleveland's west side and in Columbus, formerly worked in visual merchandising at Higbee's:

> At Higbee's, they always ran this big red runner up the center aisle at Christmastime and we'd change all the lights over—the counter lights, the jewelry cases and the makeup cases. All the shades would become red. It was fast. And then we would do the boughs up the center. Also, the big Higbee boughs came down off of every elevator. And then we would do the boughs up the center. —*Joe Valenti*

A DRAMATIC ENTRANCE

During the 1960s, as soon as you walked into Higbee's from Euclid Avenue you'd see the chandeliers, the ornaments, garlands, and trees. The little wooden escalator went halfway up to the mezzanine, where there was an imported food shop. Those skinny wooden escalators reappeared on higher floors, and a tube system was used to send messages, to see if they had your size. At the time Higbee's did not have cash registers on the floor: they wrote up your order and you had the little metal plate with your name and signature on it, and your plate number. Then your plate, cash, or check went into a tube. In half a minute, it would come back with a receipt and change, and it was always right. Coming from the Terminal Tower into Higbee's basement, you went by the malted stand. They were sold in real glasses. You started your day at the malted stand; everybody wanted one.

In 1964, Higbee's had a train ride on the toy floor, and you got a present at the end if your parents paid an extra quarter. I got one—after much screaming and crying. Mine was a tattoo, the kind that you got wet, and smacked on your arm for a little while, then peeled off. It was red, green, and blue. —*Bunny Sullivan Trepal*

THRILL OF THE GRILLE

One of my favorite memories of Christmas in Cleveland is coming downtown each year and seeing the decorated Christmas storefronts in the Higbee's building on Public Square, followed by lunch at the Silver Grille. I just remember always ordering the chicken pot pie—it arrived each time in a little cardboard oven. —*Lynne McLaughlin*

RUDOLPH'S NOT ON IT:
The Santa Breakfast Menu
from Higbee's Westgate.

SACK TIME: Children could
shop for their parents at
Higbee's Twigbee Shop.

"I got one—after much screaming and crying."

A KID'S EYE VIEW OF DOWNTOWN SHOPPING

What I remember most about going shopping downtown with my mother was her telling me to put my hands behind my back and not touch anything. At eye level, I got to see a lot of kneecaps and coats brushing against my face.

I remember going to the Silver Grille when I was older because it was a special thing. It was a great place, probably way over my taste buds at the time—the chicken pot pie. I probably never appreciated what the Silver Grille was all about as a kid. You knew you were in a grown-up place, and again, because of the time period, you knew you had to behave or something very bad could happen to you: You'd never get to go back. —*John Awarski*

DOWNTOWN DINING

At least three times, my mom and I went downtown shopping at Christmastime. I know it was three different times, because I remember going to three different places to eat lunch. I was probably seven, eight, and nine years old. I don't remember a lot about the actual shopping, but I remember the May Company store and Higbee's, with all the perfume counters. I remember how amazing department stores were back then, and I remember walking down the street, looking in the windows, and eating lunch.

NOSES ON WINDOWS:
A 1955 Higbee's
Christmas window.

LUNCH IS IN RANGE: Many families made
it a tradition to stop at the Silver Grille for lunch
after Christmas shopping at Higbee's.

"It was the first time I was ever in a fancy ladies' room."

At the Silver Grille, I had Welsh rarebit. I remember the fish pond in the middle of the restaurant. It was the first time I was ever in a fancy ladies' room. It was wonderful being able to spend time with my mom.

Once, we went to Otto Moser's on East 4th Street. My mom even had a beer, which surprised me because I don't remember her drinking. I remember seeing all the pictures on the wall, really famous people who had eaten there. Later, when I looked back on it, I thought, 'What a great place to take a kid.' With the dark wood, I thought I was in a nightclub.

I remember sitting at The Mayflower Cafeteria and seeing the mural on the wall, the saying about the doughnut: 'As you wander on through life, brother, whatever be your goal, keep your eyes upon the doughnut and not upon the hole.' —*Kathleen Cerveny*

THE TWIGBEE SHOP

Higbee's Twigbee Shop often figured into the trips downtown, where children could shop on their own.

We had five girls—Debbie, Susan, Judith, Laura, and Lisa. We would get them up in them morning and put on the starched crinoline slips under their beautiful full-skirt dresses. You would not go anywhere without your white gloves and dress-up shoes. . . . Their hair was curled the night before, in preparation for the big adventure.

The windows in each store displayed a mechanical wonderland, each depicting its own message of Christmas. Everyone was in awe of the windows. Higbee's had a train ride through a beautiful tunnel with images on either side. Only kids could go into the Twigbee Shop to buy their mom and dad a Christmas gift. They were so excited. When I think of it now, the clerks were saints, patiently waiting while the kids made this so-important decision.

There were many treasures—memories to warm the heart, memories to bring joy to those who shared them, memories that last a lifetime, and, in time, memories that only books can bring back. They were special times, with our loving, special family and we were—and are—very blessed. —*Patricia Harrison*

Higbee's had a store inside of the store, with small doors that were just about four feet high. It was like a miniature castle, but the doors were only for children to go in—no adults allowed. I remember, we couldn't wait. The fathers were all outside, and in the boomer years, you're probably talking about a hundred children at a time waiting to go into this great little castle where you could Christmas shop. For fathers, there was every Christmas tie imaginable, low cost. For mothers, there were cookie cutters and knick-knacks. You could make your own decision about what to buy for your parents. But who financed that? Your parents. —*Christopher G. Axelrod*

While in graduate school, another Clevelander worked at various jobs in Higbee's during the Christmas rush.

I assisted in the Twigbee Shop, where children could enter through a tiny Tudor door to buy presents. Most came with only a dollar to spend, and the selection was limited at that price point. I recall ringing up quite a few travel sewing kits and sample-sized flagons of English Leather. —*Joe Valencic*

TRAINS AND THE EAT TREAT

In 1950 or 1951, I remember the adventure of going downtown. We lived on East 155th Street, so my dad would run us up to the Shaker rapid and we'd take it downtown. That was another thrill, waiting for the Shaker rapid. We would get on at Avalon, and take it down into the bowels of the Cleveland Terminal. It was always exciting—a mysterious dark area where the trains would go, and the seemingly endless cave. Part of the fascination of the whole downtown adventure was the train ride down there.

Our shopping routine was Higbee's, May Company, then Taylor's, Halle's, and Sterling-Lindner. Somewhere along the line, we had lunch, either at the Silver Grille or at Mills, the cafeteria on Euclid Avenue. I just loved their biscuits and chicken. It was always so great, and you were able to eat upstairs and look down at all the people.

Higbee's was always elaborately decorated. It seemed that no area or space was left unadorned. It was just incredible, and again, the anticipation of going up to the toy department on the elevators was really great. As a kid, it seemed like the toy department went on and on. I suppose Higbee's was my favorite toy department. They seemed to have a bigger variety of stuff, and a great train area, which was also of major interest to me. —*Dennis Gaughan*

**WISH
FULFILLMENT**

PROMOTING CHRISTMAS

All the beautiful trimmings and exciting Christmas promotions at downtown department stores didn't just happen. Those shopping details you remember—the advertisements, the catalogs, and the shopping bags—were in the

THAT'S A WRAP

HELLO MY NAME IS:
May Company employee
name tag for Christmas

VALUE ADDED:
May Company Merchant
of Value trading stamps.

PLAY BOOKS

works months before Christmas. Artist Bonnie Jacobson worked in several department store advertising departments, designing Christmas shopping bags, ads, catalogs, and menus for Christmas for department stores:

> I worked at Higbee's from 1954 to the sixties. I did ad layouts for fashion and home furnishings, and things like the design and artwork for the Santa Menu at Higbee's Silver Grille. Later, I freelanced at Halle's, The May Company, and Taylor's, doing layout for ads and also finished art. I remember doing a square-shaped ad for a gift certificate, maybe for Higbee's. We really wanted to find themes, and then would use that typeface on all the Christmas ads.
>
> For newspaper ads, we started thinking about them several months ahead. We got the layout assignment and did the ad, then it was copied on the Ozalid machine and run around the store for each buyer's approval. Then we did the finished work. That was my first job out of art school. I ran the Ozalid machine—a blueprint machine like a mangle—and ran proofs around the store. After a month of this, the art director promoted me to doing layouts. —*Bonnie Jacobson*

MAY COMPANY

Whether for its playroom, or the fact that it gave Eagle Stamps that customers could paste into books and redeem for merchandise, May Company had many fans. Its Public Square location made it convenient for bus and rapid transit riders, too.

THE MEANING OF MEMORIES

It's probably a good thing I wasn't born in the '40s or I would have morphed *A Christmas Story* into my own Cleveland Christmas memories by now. However, there are moments in the iconic movie that are very reminiscent of my own youth. To be born in the '50s and raised in the '60s in a middle-class family meant that nothing much happened.

It is difficult to describe the simplicity of those years to the current generation. It is the scarcity of material possessions, the absence of media and ubiquitous electronic communication devices that make my generation's Christmas memories so unique.

My memories, I am sure, are almost exactly like those of all the children of my era—those of us fortunate enough to have parents who took the time to carry out all the relatively new traditions of an American Christmas.

How unique is a Mr. Jingeling? The *Captain Penny* show he appeared on? The enormous Sterling-Lindner tree with soccer ball-sized ornaments?

Animated figures in store windows? The '40s and '50s were glory days. Downtown Cleveland was a shopping destination before malls appeared.

My great Aunt Irene worked at the May Company. She was the only person I knew with a connection to downtown—the place of buses spewing gas fumes and people of color I had never seen in my east side suburb. (I was also quite impressed that she had Dorothy Fuldheim for a neighbor.)

At Christmas my mother would dress me up in my best dress and patent leather shoes and we rode the bus downtown so my mother could shop. We would meet Irene in her May Company office cubicle and I would be ushered off to a playroom with strangers who would look after me while my mom shopped. (Horrors!) I can still picture the playroom as a scary, dark cavernous space.

There is one distinct memory I have of my own shopping. I had to return a gift and was allowed to choose another. I remember visiting one of the downtown stores and becoming completely overwhelmed at the sight of shelves upon shelves of dolls. Dolls! My favorite thing in the world. Never in my young life had I faced such a decision. The doll I chose was an angel in a pink dress with wings. That's all. But why is that image of a wall of dolls still stuck in my mind from so long ago? Because of the sparseness of images our minds held in those decades. The abundance and onslaught of visual information that children now know from birth was missing. Therefore, every new experience was formidable and memorable. Few memories were made from movies or television—they were made from real experiences.

Standing on a sidewalk in blustery Public Square to see mechanical characters in a store window would hardly be a destination now, but then, oh yes, it was a thing of beauty. Christmas shopping at Twigbee's with our few dollars or coins is nothing to the amount of time children can spend at Walmart.

And Mr. Jingeling? What a weird old guy! Can you imagine treasuring a cardboard key? Yet we did, and life was grand. —*Diane Vogel Ferri*

MAKING THE TRIP FROM MENTOR

Each year our family made a pilgrimage from Mentor to downtown Cleveland shortly after Thanksgiving. Piling into the car and driving to the Windermere rapid station, we boarded the train and glued our faces to the windows and watched as the east side rolled by, eventually to be deposited in the bowels of the Terminal Tower. We went up the ramp to the street level on Public Square and emerged, blinking, into the cold morning air, snowflakes slowly drifting in front of our eyes. A handful of carolers greeted us as Salvation Army Santas hopefully rang their bells. The unmistakable smell of Morrow's Nut House welcomed us to the city.

HANGING OUT DOWNTOWN: Ornaments decorated the Prospect Avenue side of the May Company building.

YOU CAN ALWAYS GO DOWNTOWN

Shopping options downtown in the 1950s ranged from dime stores to department stores, and it seems that the kids of Cleveland visited just about all of them when they were on Christmas shopping excursions with their parents. A downtown merchants' ad that appeared in the *Cleveland News*, December 12, 1955, listed the addresses of many of the stores Baby Boomers remember:

- Bailey's Department Store, Ontario and Prospect

- Taylor & Sons, 630 Euclid Ave.

- Halle Brothers, 1228 Euclid Ave.

- Sterling-Lindner (Sterling-Lindner-Davis in 1955 ads), Euclid Ave. at E. 13th St.

- May Company, 158 Euclid Ave.

- Higbee's, 100 Public Sq.

The big downtown department stores weren't the only places to shop, of course. There were other downtown shops, dime stores, suburban stores, malls, and discount stores around town.

MAKING THE ROUNDS: The May Company play area, 1948.

DECKING THE HALLE'S, 1959

BACK IT UP UNDER THE TREE

PRESSING CHARGES: Charge-A-Plates were what we used before charge cards.

The big department stores were all frequented, and each had its own offerings. Of course, each had its own 'Santa's helper.' Halle's boasted Mr. Jingeling, whose direct link to Santa was not established, though he had the bona fide credential of being on TV every night at the conclusion of *Captain Penny*. The approach to his throne was via a short miniature train ride through a tunnel of wrapped presents whereupon one emerged to be greeted by his helper, the Play Lady.

The May Company possibly had the most interesting and extensive toy department, though its charm was significantly rivaled by the gigantic Sterling-Lindner Christmas tree and its many ornaments. At dinnertime, Higbee's offered the Silver Grille, where their child's dinner could be served on a small cardboard stove, which could be taken home for a souvenir.

The train ride home was always a tired but exhilarating journey. The lights, sounds, and wonders of downtown shopping danced through our dreams, only slightly overtaken by the anticipation of the Big Day that lay ahead. —*William Small*

GIFT CERTIFICATES

The downtown department stores were always beautifully decorated but we couldn't wait until the day after Christmas, when we could take our new fifteen-dollar gift certificate and shop the after-Christmas sale in the May Company basement. We would shop all day. —*Helen Wirt*

CLEVELAND CHRISTMASES OFFERED LIFE LESSONS

I think back now and realize that many of my fondest Christmas memories came with valuable lessons for the future. First, there was the exciting annual trip downtown on the RTA, where I learned the fine art of observing others—a useful skill for any writer. The creaky wooden department store escalators taught me to face my fears. My favorite store was the May Company because we'd get dropped off in this big children's play room so parents could shop without distractions. Here I learned how to play well with others, that running in circles makes you dizzy, and not to ask Mom what was in those packages she carried when she returned. And while I was forced to wait in line for what seemed like an eternity to see Santa and Mr. Jingeling, I must admit now, I never acquired the knack for being patient.

Then there was the thrill of decorating the Christmas tree—never sooner than two weeks before the big day. Every year my brother would yell at me for not taking my time and placing the tinsel on 'just right.' But it ultimately taught me to take pride in what I did—perhaps the greatest lesson of all. —*Deanna R. Adams, author of* Confessions of a Not-So-Good Catholic Girl *and other books*

HALLE BROTHERS

Whether you walked to 12th and Euclid or took the Halle's shuttle bus, the animated Christmas windows were worth the trip. Once inside the store, not only was Santa Claus holding court, but beginning in 1956, Mr. Jingeling was there, too, on Halle's seventh floor.

THE KEYS TO IT ALL

They gave away the Mr. Jingeling keys in the store. They were in the Santa Claus department, and Mr. Jingeling would just hang around a little bit and talk to the kids. But Mr. Jingeling got so big, so fast, that he became a real major part of the downtown Christmas. —*Ron Newell*

HAPPY HALLE DAYS: Halle's offered not only the chance to visit Santa and Mr. Jingeling, but also a treasure house of gifts.

POWER SHOPPING

BEHIND THE SCENES

"Halle's was a wonderful store, like a family store. In high school, I worked as a gift wrapper and an elevator operator. They trained me to gift wrap—how to tie bows and measure the paper so you didn't waste any. It was nice money because you'd get tips, too; I didn't ask if I should take them. As an elevator operator, I was so excited because I got to get my hair done at the beauty parlor there. The drawback was that I had to wear old lady ox-fords. The customers were usually in a good mood, and I liked kids. You met a lot of people there—and cute boys." *—Ellen Dunlay*

SHOPPING WITHOUT STOPPING:
The scene at Halle's during Christmas season, 1963.

JUST A FEW SCENTS MORE: Last-minute shopper at Halle's perfume counter, Christmas Eve, 1953.

AN ELEVATING EXPERIENCE AT HALLE'S

You'd go to the elevators and push a button and the doors would roll open. There was the operator, always dressed very, very nicely, to haul you where you wanted to go. *—Virginia Meil*

STERLING-LINDNER-DAVIS

It was a hike to Euclid and 13th Street from Public Square, but well worth it. The rewards included the spectacle of the giant Sterling-Lindner tree, and being able to play in the Toyland area. While each year's Christmas tree was different, the statistics were always impressive. In 1948, the tree in the store's Great Court was forty-five feet tall. Other years, it ranged from fifty to sixty feet tall. The sixty-foot-tall tree was decorated with fifteen hundred ornaments, a thousand yards of tinsel, and sixty pounds of icicles.

FRANCIS THE TALKING MULE AT STERLING-LINDNER-DAVIS

My sister Darlene remembers that one of the most fascinating things for her as a kid was the chute where a toy, or a gift, would come down. The gift would always be matched for your gender and your age. She said it was always magical as a young kid, how they could know who you were. It came down the chute at an angle and she said it was like this gift was coming from the North Pole.

It was in the Toyland area, and I remember it as large and green, with a chute probably at a forty-five-degree angle. You were always curious, and tried to look and see through the hole, to see who was back there doing that. The impression was that the elves were all back there, preparing all these gifts. The other stores had similar set-ups, but I don't remember anything quite as unusual as Sterling-Lindner. —*Dennis Gaughan*

PUTTING UP THE STERLING-LINDNER TREE

To me, the Sterling-Lindner tree was the epitome of Christmas. I was working on the Halle's window displays, and our windows were directly across the street from the Sterling-Lindner entrance. To put the tree up, they would block off the street in front of us, and crowds would form around the barricades. Then this huge truck would come down the street with a monstrous tree and unload it. They would have to take the doors off to load it in. They also had buckets to lower the guys who trimmed it. It was fantastic. We'd stop our work and watch them put that tree in there, and then we'd go over to see it. You know, display people went around to every store. We enjoyed all of it. There was a sort of pleasant competition between the stores. It was never, 'I hate this, I hate that.' We were a group. But watching the Sterling-Lindner tree go in, that in itself was an event. —*Ron Newell*

YULE MULE

The following is a description of a young family's visit in 1951 to the Toyland at Sterling-Lindner-Davis with its merry-go-round and Francis the Talking Mule attractions. The description was published in the *Cleveland News:*

GAIL ENJOYS HER TOUR OF TOYLAND
We chose the store we visited because it had a merry-go-round to please small customers who dropped in to make their Christmas selections. Gail held onto the colorful horse 'all by herself' and proudly gave the young attendant her orange ticket when he came by to collect . . .

She met Francis the Talking Mule—and it was quite a meeting. Gail stood looking up at the huge stuffed animal with amazement. She was simply speechless.

After standing silently before the animal for some time she suddenly turned to us and said, 'Ohh, see the big horsie.' Then she pointed to his flapping jaw and his eyes, which rolled about in his head.

When the huge 'horsie' said, 'Hello, Gail,' she was really surprised. She laughed and called back, 'Hello, horsie.'

CLAUS ENCOUNTER: This poster was displayed in the side window of Woolworth's on East 4th Street downtown.

PIN CODE: Kids who visited Francis the Talking Mule at Sterling-Lindner Davis got this souvenir pin.

TOP TREE: Sterling-Lindner Christmas tree postcards.

FOR FANS OF THE BIG TREE: Sterling-Lindner's 60-foot-tall Christmas tree was decorated with 60 pounds of icicles, 1,500 ornaments, and draped with 1,000 yards of tinsel.

'I'm no horsie, I'm a mule,' the huge animal said in a pleasant voice. So Gail obligingly said, 'Hello, mule . . .'

It pleased Gail when Francis told her he had a toy for her and a wrapped package came sliding down a chute into her hands. But not until after we had left did she think about investigating the contents . . . A dish of ice cream in a nearby drug store ended our afternoon of fun.

—*Janice Fleming Ghetia, "Life With Baby," November 15, 1951*

WINDOWS ON THE PAST

Clevelanders were wowed by the downtown department windows at Christmas. Ron Newell, who was a window display designer for Halle Brothers, worked at the store from 1956 until Halle's closed in 1982. He later became Halle's Special Events Director. He discusses the philosophy of Christmas windows, and what made them so special.

For some of the smaller stores like Bonwit Teller, animation really wasn't their thing. Each store sort of had its own color code, or its own palette. Some used aluminum Christmas trees when they came out in the sixties. Some went very, very avant garde and did extremely far-out windows for Christmas—and they worked. It didn't matter what style you chose; as long as everything worked together, you had something.

Higbee's had its own style of doing windows, and so did Halle's. A window has to have something for everybody when they look into it. You have to have somebody doing something—whether it's the little guy hammering,

MORE DOWNTOWN STORES

W. T. Grant, 240 Euclid Ave.

S.S. Kresge, 216 Euclid Ave. and 402 Euclid Ave.

F.W. Woolworth, 306 Euclid Ave. and 1317 Euclid Ave.

Richman Brothers, 736 Euclid Ave. and 2097 Ontario St.

Newman Stern, 1740 E. 12th St.

B.R. Baker, 1001 Euclid Ave.

Bonwit Teller, 1331 Euclid Ave.

Burrows, 419 Euclid Ave. and 1605 Euclid Ave.

Cowell & Hubbard, Euclid Ave. at E. 13th St.

Hobby House, 800 Huron Rd.

Harry Jacobson, 413 Euclid Ave.

Lane Bryant, 1021 Euclid Ave.

Milgrim's, 1310 Huron Rd.

DRAMATIC DISPLAY:
Higbee's Nutcracker Window, 1979

MAKING THE SCENE:
Ron Newell (right) with
Christmas window model

GOOD SPORTS AT CHRISTMAS

Clevelanders have sports on their minds throughout the year, so it's not surprising to find Christmas connections. In 1935, athlete Jesse Owens distributed Christmas baskets to Cleveland families, just months before winning four Olympic Gold Medals in 1936 in Berlin. In 1950 and 1972, fans watched the Cleveland Browns play in Christmas Eve games. During the Christmas shopping season in 1964, local football fans headed downtown to the May Co. Book Shop, where Jim Brown was autographing copies of his new book, *Off My Chest: One of the Greatest Athletes of All Time Tells the Story of his Life—On and Off the Field*. The book was written with Myron Cope and sold for $4.95. In 1980, locals were singing a special Christmas carol, "The Twelve Days of a Cleveland Browns Christmas," in anticipation of the AFC Divisional Playoffs.

RUNNING AHEAD OF SCHEDULE: In 1935, soon-to-be Olympic gold medalist Jesse Owens took the time to distribute gift baskets at Christmas.

DOWNTOWN DISPLAYS: Halle's and Higbee's had many popular window displays that included *A Christmas Carol* and *The Wizard of Oz*.

and over there a little guy climbing, and over here a little guy stirring the paint—so that when you look, you see a story. You tell a story in the window. Another thing is that window displays are like what headlines are to a newspaper. The window is the headline. When you stand across the street and look at my windows, you've got to see a headline that says, 'Buddy, come on in.' Part of the job for the display person was to draw people in. —*Ron Newell*

NOSE PRINTS ON WINDOWS

My favorite window displays were Halle's. They were fantasy. The people who put those windows together, for them it was a privilege. Do you know how you can tell the best window displays? You can tell them at night, when you're inside the store and the lights are on. What do you see? Nose prints. A great window has nose prints, and it has them on all levels. I've had window displays where I've looked in there and could tell it was a little kid, and an adult. That, to me, means you've succeeded. I think probably the greatest lost art of the holidays is the art of window dressing. —*Steve Presser*

FAVORITE CHRISTMAS WINDOW DISPLAYS

I remember going downtown to see the wonderful windows. Halle's department store always had the best of them. May Company only had them up for a short while. —*Bill Hixson*

ANIMATED DISPLAYS

The great thing was the window displays that all the department stores had, standing there looking at the animatronic things, or whatever they were called back then, and watching the train sets going around. Literally, we spent probably ten minutes but it felt like hours, just watching the windows. There was one window—I can't remember which store—with a manikin kind of thing with a wand that would go over a little piece of wood on the window. You'd hear this tapping noise, and just watch it, thinking, 'When is the window going to break?' I knew if I had tapped the window, it would have broken. This thing tapped the window all day and it hadn't broken yet. —*John Awarski*

ARE WE RUSSIAN THE HOLIDAYS?: Over the years, Halle's windows featured Gift-Giving Traditions from all over the world, including Italy, the Netherlands, and Russia.

REDEEMING VALUE: Bailey's and Fries & Schuele were among the stores offering savings stamps.

YULE PAY FOR THAT

In the pre-credit card days, Clevelanders still had many options besides forking over cash for their Christmas purchases. They redeemed books of trading stamps, handed over their department store Charge-A-Plates at the cash register, joined Christmas Clubs at their banks, and put gifts in layaway to make time payments.

In the 1950s, May Company was giving out Eagle Stamps. When customers made a purchase, they were given trading stamps at the register, based on the amount of money they had spent. The idea was to paste the stamps into savings books and later redeem them for merchandise. Bailey's gave out Merchant Savings Stamps. Other retailers offered S&H Green Stamps.

DECK THE MALLS: The 20-foot-tall Santa at May Company, Parmatown Mall.

SHOPPING AROUND IN 1955

Gray Drug Store advertised the Corday Eau de Toilette Wardrobe (Toujours Moi, Fame, Zigone, and Jet scents nestled in a satin box) for $3.

Halle's was advertising The Betty Crocker Bake Set with 12 baking mixes for $4.95; the Heddi Stroller Doll with jointed knees sold for $7.95.

Giant Tiger was selling Christmas wreaths for 89 cents each. Giant Tiger had store locations at 624 E. 185 St., 11001 Lorain Ave., 13511 Miles Rd., 1939 W. 25 St., 8301 Euclid Ave., 3326 Warren Rd., and 6000 Brookpark Rd. at Pearl Rd.

Hobby House priced its HO Beginner's Electric Train Set at $24.88.

ON TRACK FOR CHRISTMAS: The Christmas train at Parmatown, 1979.

Cleveland department store window themes ranged from Higbee's Charles Dickens-inspired scenes to Halle's Christmas Around the World series.

We researched every country to find out their Christmas traditions and what they called Santa Claus. Then we did Christmastimes in the history of the United States, including Christmas on a wagon train. There was also a whole series of windows based on Mr. Jingeling in different sketches. One was Mr. Jingeling in Space, and he was floating around with a bubble on his head, because everybody thought spacemen wore bubbles. We put a plastic bubble over his head, and he looked great. Mr. Jingeling was very versatile. I think we even put him in the wagon train, and dressed him as wagon master. In one window he was a butler. We took some liberties. He still had the wig and you knew it was him. —*Ron Newell*

CHRISTMAS IN MARCH

At Halle's, work on the Christmas window displays started in March. We set up the themes at meetings where everybody was involved, including fashion and display. Once the theme was developed, we started in on the Christmas animated windows. We would have a meeting with all the artistic people in the display department and sketch out the window, based on the theme and whatever story we wanted to tell. For each theme, we had six regular windows. Starting east, those were windows one and two, then the east opening off Euclid Avenue, then more windows and the west doorway. Also, continuing west, there was the specialty window, and the corner window right next to it that ran into Halle's Alley down the alley so it was a two-sided window. We gave each window a theme, based on the larger theme, and decided how many figures we wanted and the choreography. A lot of the research was done at the library.

The display department went to a convention in New York City held in June. We designed what we wanted the animated figures to do, and went there with all our ideas. It was like a factory—I mean, little arms and feet were hanging there. There was a standard little motor on a base. You would choose, saying, 'I want the figure to do this, and the head to bob.' Then we went in with the fashion ideas, too, whether it was to be a period piece or whatever, and they would pull the fabrics and make the clothes for the animated figures. You picked the size of the figures, too. It might be one-third life-size, one-quarter life-size, or one-half life-size. At Halle's, we used one-third life-size. The figures were about 18 to 24 inches tall. Sometimes you could reconfigure or reuse the animation the following year without having to get a new set, then we would dress them ourselves. We did a lot of things ourselves. Regardless of the period, we made the furniture ourselves. —*Ron Newell*

OUT FOR A SPIN: Two animated Victorian skating figures from a Halle's window display.

MATCH THE ADVERTISING SLOGAN WITH THE STORE

1. "The Big Store"

2. "Treasure House of Gifts"

3. "A Gift From _____ Means More"

4. "World of Toys"

5. "Ohio's Largest Toyland"

Answers:

TAKING IN ALL THE SIGHTS

On the way up Euclid Avenue to the stores, you could stop into Woolworth's and Kresge's. It was one of those that had an escalator that went downstairs and fluorescent lights on the white plastic sides of the escalator. The toys were on the downstairs level. It was like a feast, seeing what toys would be down there, and it was always very colorful. Of course, in the dime stores there was no Santa giving anything out. —*Dennis Gaughan*

MORE STORES

Captain Penny always used to mention Fries and Schuele, which sounded like a cornucopia of toys and bicycles, but it was somewhere on the far-flung west side. In the 1960s, the downtown

CALLING ALL MALL-CRAWLERS: Severance Center Shoppers, 1964.

UNCLE BILL'S
IS FOR THE PEOPLE
TV LISTINGS
Sun. December 1st thru
Sat. December 7th, 1974

SANTA'S SUPER SALE!
Starts
Wednesday, December 4th
Watch your Mail for Uncle Bill's
16-Page Color Circular for
Fantastic savings for Christmas!
Come See....Come Save!

We're for the People

BARGAIN BINGE:
Shopping the Christmas
clearance sale at May
Company, 1967.

department stores had the best and classiest toy selections. Along East 185th Street we had neighborhood stores like Woolworth's and Neisner's dime stores, and the Teddy Bear Store (mostly children's apparel) that had limited choices. Burrows was good for games. I grew up just when discount department stores were opening. They had toys and games, but not always the as-seen-on-TV name brands. These stores introduced us to cheaply made metal and plastic playthings from Japan and Korea. The stores also had a certain low-budget look: lots of linoleum, metal shelving, and fluorescent lighting sprawling. They were low-slung brick-and-glass structures that anchored a new architectural phenomenon, the suburban strip mall. No one had ever shopped like that before.

My East 185th Street neighborhood was the eastern-most shopping area for folks as far away as Lake County. With the advent of suburban strip malls, the shops in my neighborhood shopping district began shutting their doors. On the east side, there were Giant Tiger, Uncle Bill's, Joe Norban's, and Silverman's. I recall not especially liking the merchandise. These stores were okay for buying Christmas gifts for people you didn't particularly care to spend on, but you didn't want to knowingly get gifts from them. You could always tell toys, games, and clothing from these—they had this plasticky discount store smell. —*Joe Valencic*

1/2 PRICE   CHRISTMAS CARDS WRAPPING PAPER TRIM-A-TREE ITEMS

The Arts of Christmas in Cleveland

Our Christmas culture is evident in plays and ballets, music, and the books we read—especially events with a Cleveland connection. Consider The Cleveland Play House's holiday season performances of *A Christmas Carol* by Charles Dickens, the traditional Cleveland Orchestra Christmas Concerts, and The Cleveland Ballet performances of *The Nutcracker*.

During its 65th season, The Cleveland Play House presented *A Christmas Carol* by Charles Dickens, a new adaptation by Doris Baizle that was directed by William Rhys. The play ran from November 28, 1980, through January 4, 1981. The set and costumes, designed by Charles Berliner, were an integral part of the play. Cleveland Play House Resident Scenic Designer Richard Gould, who did the lighting, and Design Supervisor Estelle Painter, the costume assistant to the designer, share their recollections of working on *A Christmas Carol*.

A MEMORABLE METAMORPHOSIS

The whole shape of the show was unique, and the idea of the piece itself was that a rag-tag gypsy acting company, actors and personnel, were touring around doing this production. At the beginning of the piece, the actors were introduced as their acting company membership characters. That is, there was a leading man, the leading lady, an ingénue, and the young leading man. Also there was a stage manager, a costume mistress, a director and a prop boy, and four or five company members who were extras. As the play developed, they all became characters in *A Christmas Carol* and took things out of a trunk to produce the piece. As they went from their theater persona into their character, there was a very obvious kind of metamorphosis. The stage manager, played by Wayne S. Turney, became Scrooge. The director became Marley. The young leading man became Bob Cratchit, and the prop boy, played by Allan Byrne, became Tiny Tim. After the first year, Evie McElroy always played the costume mistress. Sharon Bicknell played the ingénue, the costume mistress's daughter.

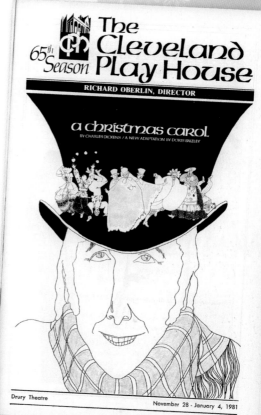

A DICKENS OF A TIME: The Cleveland Play House offered *A Christmas Carol* during its 65th season.

"The whole shape of the show was unique."

WQAL SOUNDS OF CHRISTMAS: 1983 was the eleventh year of WQAL's 30-hour Christmas music program from 6 p.m. on Christmas Eve through midnight on Christmas Day.

I think the importance of this production was that it was not the traditional *Christmas Carol*, but a very different, very simple version. It was very accessible to young kids. After doing something for four or five years, anybody could get a little cynical about it, but Evie McElroy said she really loved doing it every Christmas because of the way audiences responded to it. If you had to work your holiday, it was a very, very, nice way to be doing it. It was very physical, with some mime, some songs, and a lot of joy. The magic moments, the visual magic moments, that came out of the design were important moments of Scrooge's transformations. Keeping it that simple was what made it so effective. —*Estelle Painter*

BEHIND THE SCENES AT *A CHRISTMAS CAROL*

The play had been produced once before it came to The Play House, but not in that particular form. The premise was that it was a little touring company that came with this great big box with all the props and costumes, and everything evolved from that huge trunk. When Charles Berliner, who works out of California, designed the magic box, it was designed for the 77th Street Theater. Because the box was so big, when it was moved to 86th Street to the Drury Theater, the techies had to haul it down Euclid Avenue on dollies because it couldn't fit in the truck. Charles Berliner also did the costumes. His drawings were very detailed and you really had to follow them to the letter, but it was a huge hit. —*Richard Gould*

AN AUDIENCE MEMBER RECALLS *A CHRISTMAS CAROL* OF THE PAST

The version of *A Christmas Carol* that The Play House did was transformational theater. The stage was set for something other than the play. I remember Wayne Turney being Scrooge. In the play, I think the actors for *A Christmas Carol* didn't show up. The stage folks had to put the play on, and none of them knew how to do it. Before your eyes, with a little bit of grease paint and turning his coat inside out to become a different kind of coat, Wayne Turney was transformed into Scrooge. And a table cloth turned over to become a bedspread, or something a ghost wore. It's the essence of what theater is about. It was really magical, and there were only a few characters. —*Kathleen Cerveny*

It was really magical, and there were only a few characters.

BENEATH THE TREE: The battle scene featuring children in The Cleveland Ballet's performance of *The Nutcracker* at the State Theatre at PlayhouseSquare.

THE GREAT LAKES SHAKESPEARE FESTIVAL

A Child's Christmas in Wales

WORLD PREMIERE
THE OHIO THEATRE
DECEMBER - JANUARY
1982 - 1983

PLAYHOUSE SQUARE
CLEVELAND, OHIO

CHRISTMAS IN WALES: The Great Lakes Shakespeare Festival world premiere of Dylan Thomas' *A Child's Christmas in Wales* took place at The Ohio Theatre, December-January 1982-83, at Playhouse Square. This holiday entertainment by Jeremy Brooms and Adrian Mitchell listed Vincent Dowling as Producing Director, and was directed by Clifford Williams.

"My theory is that the singing of songs and the telling of tales, which is what we do at Christmas, is the only fit way for humans to communicate with each other."—D.J. Thomas

A LOCAL TRADITION:
Dennis Nahat and
Nanette Glushak in
The Cleveland Ballet's
Christmas favorite,
The Nutcracker.

JUST US MICE: The Cleveland
Ballet performances of *The
Nutcracker* thrilled audiences at the
State Theatre at PlayhouseSquare.

OTHER CHRISTMAS CAROLS

We have a family tradition to this day where we go to see the Great Lakes Theater version of *A Christmas Carol* every year. I love the various versions of it. I collect filmed versions of *A Christmas Carol*—any movie adaptation or animated version of the Dickens classic. I have forty-seven different ones so far. —*Bob Burford*

BLACK NATIVITY

As a third grader, my daughter Kaitlin Noel Smith was an angel in *Black Nativity* at Karamu House. The biggest memory that stands out for me is going from Berea to Karamu every night for two and a half months for rehearsals and performances. The night of dress rehearsal, we left Karamu and it was a terrible snowstorm. We hadn't known it was going on, and driving home, there were no street lights. We both agreed it was the spookiest, scariest night. I also remember Terence Greene, the principal dancer for *Black Nativity*. He was just incredible, the way he was with the kids. They were so young and he taught them about being in love with their bodies, and feeling good about themselves. All the "angels" were girls of different ages and sizes. He had an incredible warmth, so the kids weren't frightened. He told them how lucky the people in the audience would be to get to see them on stage. He totally reversed the idea of being afraid to be onstage. Another thing that wasn't lost on me: In a world that pictures all things all white all the time, it was wonderful for my daughter to see the many hues of color and know they are all beautiful, because when you see angels pictured, they're rarely pictured as angels of color. —*Katie Smith*

HAVING A BALLET MERRY CHRISTMAS

Clevelanders continue to wax nostalgic about productions of Dennis Nahat's version of *The Nutcracker*, especially the Cleveland Ballet performances that began at the State Theatre at PlayhouseSquare in 1984. Arts advocate Barbara S. Robinson explains: "There were previous productions of *The Nutcracker*, but its full glory was really when it was presented at the State Theatre, with the tech facilities and the size of the stage that it had. It was a full-blown production. A season that began as a week or ten days at the State ended up being extended through to New Years, all the time, and we had full audiences. The State's capacity was approximately two thousand."

Barbara Robinson discusses why *The Nutcracker* inspired such devotion:

FROM PAGE TO PLAY: THE CLEVELAND CONNECTION

Dick Feagler's "Aunt Ida" column has become a Cleveland Christmas classic since its first appearance in *The Plain Dealer* in 1993. In the column, he reminisces about a post–World War II family gathering at his Aunt Ida's house, "not far from the steel mills." In 2006, The Huntington Playhouse in Bay Village staged the world premiere of the play, "Christmas at Aunt Ida's," written by Anne McEvoy and adapted from Dick Feagler's column. The play was directed by Tom Meyrose.

At Karamu House, *Black Nativity* has been a perennial favorite since it was first performed in Cleveland in the early 1980s. Written by Harlem Renaissance poet/playwright/author Langston Hughes—a Karamu alumnus and graduate of Cleveland's Central High School—the play was first performed in 1961 off Broadway.

CHANNELING CHRISTMAS IN CLEVELAND

December 17, 1947, was the date of the inaugural broadcast for WEWS Channel 5 in Cleveland. That first broadcast was of the annual *Cleveland Press* Christmas party with Jimmy Stewart at Public Hall. That Christmas connection was later underscored when the first Mr. Jingeling show was broadcast on WEWS a decade later, in November 1957.

Meanwhile, on KYW TV-3, Barnaby (Linn Sheldon) came out with the Christmas 45 rpm record, "Boofo Goes Where Santa Goes," released on Cosmic Records in 1958. The first line, followed by a spoken intro by Barnaby and accompanied by Boofo's barking, is "Boofo lies at Santa's feet all summer, winter long/ He keeps his toes so nice and warm 'cause Santa's socks are torn." The flip side, "Rabbits Have a Christmas," begins, "Rabbits have a Christmas, just like you and me / Rabbits have a Christmas. They even have a tree." A 1997 book, *Boofo: The Dog That Goes Where Santa Goes*, was written by Clevelanders Joseph P. King and E. Del Thomas and illustrated by Dick Dugan.

I think there are two things. One is that *The Nutcracker* is generally a family-oriented ballet. It tells a story, and coincides with the Christmas season. It is very easily acceptable as a tradition for the entire family. I think that the Cleveland Ballet form of it was highlighted by the fact that it had unusually high standards in production values—stagecraft, costumes—as well as the quality and enthusiasm of the dancers. No matter how many times they danced it, they seemed as though they were enjoying it as much themselves as the audience was enjoying it. It also had a little bit of mystery and mystique about it.

We had ticket pricing that made it available to families, so they could enjoy it as a group. All those elements I just mentioned somehow came together in one production, *The Nutcracker*. It became a Christmas tradition. I'm sure there was a continuous tradition that existed among people who saw it many, many years. It's associated with happiness, joyfulness, family tradition and Christmas spirit."

A FAMILY MEMORY OF *THE NUTCRACKER*

My daughter Jessica was at School of the Cleveland Ballet. In addition to being a caroler in *The Nutcracker* when she was smaller, she got to do things onstage, like the mice. She got to operate some of the mechanical mice that run around Clara's feet in the first act. There were no set roles for the kids—they were carolers and mice. In fact, I think there were one hundred mice the year that both my daughters were in it. —*Virginia Meil*

CHRISTMAS IS ON THE AIR

One Christmas song that comes to mind is Jose Feliciano's "Feliz Navidad." Until a certain point in time, we would actually play that every year. At Christmastime, we'd break out Bing Crosby's "White Christmas" and Elvis Presley's "I'll be Home for Christmas," Burl Ives' "Winter Wonderland," and Nat King Cole's "Chestnuts Roasting on an Open Fire," also known as "The Christmas Song." Those ballads were played for the longest period of time, surely during all my years at 3WE and maybe the first few years at WQAL. —*Larry Morrow*

JUST FOR THE RECORD: THE SOUND OF CHRISTMAS MUSIC

People in every city sing Christmas carols, but only in Cleveland do we sing Barnaby's "Boofo Goes Where Santa Goes," The "Mr. Jingeling" song and the Cleveland Browns version of "The Twelve Days of Christmas."

In 1980, after the Cleveland Browns played the Cincinnati Bengals on December 21 and won, 27-24, the Browns earned their spot in the AFC Divisional Playoffs in Cleveland on January 4, 1981. Throughout the Christmas season, as fans awaited the big day in January, Cleveland radio stations played the song, "The Twelve Days of a Cleveland Browns Christmas." The song, by Elliott, Walter, and Bennett, was sung to the tune of "The Twelve Days of Christmas."

Actually, football fans enjoyed 14 days of Christmas in 1980. Between the December 21 game in Cincinnati and the January 4, 1981, game played in Cleveland, everybody sang along with this song. The momentum and singing carried over into the New Year. However, on January 4, the heartbreaking score of that playoff game was Oakland Raiders 14, Cleveland Browns 12.

Here's what Clevelanders were singing about throughout the Christmas Season in 1980:

On the first day of Christmas, Art Modell gave to me
A Rutigliano Superbowl team (Sam Rutigliano)
Don Cockroft kicking
Brian Sipe a-passing
Alzado attacking (Lyle Alzado)
Both the Pruitts' moves (Greg Pruitt and Mike Pruitt)
Newsome a-catching (Ozzie Newsome)
Darden intercepting (Thom Darden)
The Kardiac Kids a-winning
DeLeone a-hiking (Tom DeLeone)
Doug Dieken blocking
Dave Logan leaping
The Browns in the playoffs

A BUZZARD CHRISTMAS CAROL

Cleveland had yet another favorite performance of *A Christmas Carol*—a contemporary version of the Charles Dickens classic, created and performed by the staff at radio station WMMS. Among the stars were Murray Saul as Iggy Scrooge, David Spero as David Marley, Kid Leo as Little Leo, and Matt the Cat as Matt the Cratchit. The feature was first broadcast on Christmas Eve 1975 and was repeated annually through 1985.

HOLIDAY BUZZARD: Pioneering FM radio station WMMS celebrated Christmas with ads, holiday-themed rock 'n roll tunes, and even dramatized their own take on *A Christmas Carol*.

CHRISTMAS MUSIC MEMORIES: Cleveland Orchestra recordings are local favorites.

ROCK AND ROLL

I have fond memories of Don Kriss and Rick Christyson playing "Run, Run Rudolph" in various bands, among them, The Names and Tongue Thrust—at Hennessy's and other venues during the holiday season. —*Nancy Reese*

A TREE-TRIMMING TRADITION

In our family, the tradition was to decorate the tree while watching the Cleveland Orchestra Christmas concert on television. My sister Cecilia was a member of the Cleveland Orchestra Chorus, under the direction of Robert Shaw, and we would keep an eye out to spot her on the screen. It's not Christmas without choral classics, like the 'Carol of the Bells' and 'Fum, Fum, Fum.' —*Joe Valencic*

SILVER BELLS, SILVER BELLS

You know it's Christmastime in the city when the Women's Committee of the Cleveland Orchestra begins its annual sale of Christmas bells. The tradition was started 46 years ago by the late Barbara and Arnold Schreibman of Schreibman Jewelers as a fundraiser for the Cleveland Orchestra. They sold Reed & Barton silver-plated bells engraved with the word 'Christmas' and the date. The store, located at Landerwood Plaza in Pepper Pike, closed in 2003 and the fundraiser is now a project of the Cleveland Orchestra Women's Committee. Bells are sold at Severance Hall, and at eight stores participating in the program.

Beth Schreibman Gehring describes the first year her parents launched the Silver Bells project:

I remember how hopeful they were, and how it took off. They were so excited that there were repeat customers. That year, I

BELLS WERE RINGING: Barbara and Arnold Schreibman in 1966, selling silver bells at Schreibman Jewelers during the Christmas season to raise money for the Cleveland Orchestra.

"I remember how hopeful they were, and how it took off."

think they raised something like $300. By the time we closed the store, it was $7,000 to $8,000.

We still sell the same bell today. The stated mission of the Women's Committee of the Cleveland Orchestra is education. For years, the cash provided by the Silver Bells project has helped to get kids to Severance Hall. They get to touch and play instruments—it's a real hands-on program.

ON A LIGHT NOTE

In December 1948, attendees at a Cleveland Orchestra concert found the bright side of a sudden darkness that overtook much of the city's east side, including Severance Hall, where George Szell was conducting the Cleveland Orchestra.

The blackout was a result of a fire at Cleveland Electric Illuminating Company's switch house at the Lake Shore plant at East 71st Street. *Cleveland Press* music critic Arthur Loesser described how the lights went out: "It waited to let George Szell finish conducting his delightful performance of Hayden's great E-flat Symphony to the last note before allowing Severance Hall to plunge into darkness."

However, when somebody in the darkened concert hall began to sing "O Little Town of Bethlehem," hundreds joined in and the Cleveland Orchestra began playing along. *Plain Dealer* music critic Herbert Elwell said the Orchestra was "a little timid at first." He noted that it was probably the first time in the history of symphony concerts that the audience provided part of the music. Arthur Loesser, *Cleveland Press* music critic, provided details about the carols, including "Silent Night" and "Hark! The Herald Angels Sing." Then, he wrote, "A conflict began to develop between a faction that started 'The Holly and the Ivy' and one that broke into 'It Came Upon a Midnight Clear.' The latter won by a mass action and the Orchestra stuck with the victors. Cloyd Duff's tympani could be heard in a triumphant accompaniment."

All told, the impromptu carol-singing is said to have lasted fifteen minutes before Thomas L. Sidle of the Musical Arts Association announced from the stage that the remainder of the program would be postponed until the following evening. Ticket stubs were honored at that second concert, at which time the entire program was played.

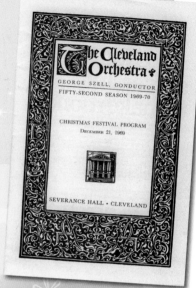

MUSIC WAS IN THE AIR: Program from the Cleveland Orchestra Christmas Festival, George Szell, Conductor, 1969.

A SUNDAY OF SONG: A 1977 caroling program at Severance Hall with Robert Page conducting the Cleveland Orchestra Chorus.

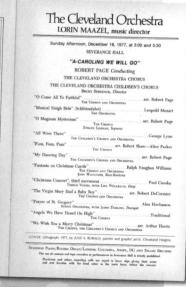

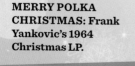

MERRY POLKA CHRISTMAS: Frank Yankovic's 1964 Christmas LP.

A DIFFERENT SPIN ON CHRISTMAS: William Lausche's lyrics for this Frank Yankovic song include the words, "There'll always be a Christmas with its mem'ries of long, long ago."

CLEVELAND-STYLE POLKA AND CHRISTMAS

What could be more fun than Christmas *and* polka music? Cleveland's local music scene has always been as diverse as the many nationalities making up the city's population. A century ago, a new style of American dance music emerged from Cleveland's working-class communities. The Cleveland-style polka was rooted in folk songs brought to the area by Slovenian immigrants, but influenced by other American music, such as jazz, blues, country, and Tin Pan Alley tunes. Accordionist Frank Yankovic, who grew up in South Collinwood, made the music swing by adding a banjo, drum set, and English lyrics. Major record labels took notice and signed him and other local polka bandleaders to national contracts. Their happy, wholesome, good-time music arrived on the scene just as GIs were returning from World War II and flocking to neighborhood dances to meet girls. By 1949 Yankovic had earned two gold records and the title of America's Polka King. Cleveland became Polka Capital of the World.

To capitalize upon his popularity, Yankovic collaborated with local composer William "Doc" Lausche to pen a couple of Christmas tunes for a Columbia release on 78 rpm. Doc, the brother of Mayor, Governor, and Senator Frank J. Lausche, was a dentist by trade with a knack for writing music and playing the piano. Since the 1920s, he had been updating Slovenian folk songs with syncopation and dance-band arrangements for Victor and Columbia recordings performed by his sister, Josephine Welf, and their friend Mary Udovich. He also sold original compositions such as "Cleveland, the Polka Town." In 1949 Doc wrote the first two Cleveland-style polka holiday numbers, "The Christmas Polka," loosely based on a Slovenian folk melody, and "There'll Always Be a Christmas," a waltz. Yankovic recorded them and the tunes soon entered the Cleveland-style polka repertoire. He vocalized with Cleveland keyboardist Buddy Griebel (still performing at 92!) on the former and with bass player Al Leslie on the latter. Both were reissued and rerecorded by Yankovic, as well as by other performers.

Yankovic released two Christmas LPs, "Christmas Party," in 1964, and, twenty years later, "Christmas Memories," produced by Steve Popovich for his Cleveland International label. Former Clevelander Joey Miskulin, Yankovic's frequent co-accordionist, now with the cowboy combo Riders in the Sky, wrote original holiday songs for the album.

As holiday broadcasts of *Polka Varieties* and yuletide dances at ethnic halls fade from memory, Yankovic's rollicking polka renditions of Christmas favorites live on through YouTube and CDs available on Amazon and at the National Cleveland-Style Polka Hall of Fame and Museum in Euclid.

—*Joe Valencic, President, National Cleveland-Style Polka Hall of Fame and Museum*

A LOOK AT CHRISTMAS BOOKS

Through the years, reading about Christmas has brought pleasure to Clevelanders.

During the 1950 Christmas season, the *Cleveland News* daily newspaper ran "Christmas Holiday," serialized fiction for adults. The story was written by author Sarah-Elizabeth Rodger, a poet and novelist whose fiction also appeared in installments in national magazines and newspaper supplements. On December 8, her story, "Christmas Holiday," was synopsized: "Three Americans meet on holiday in the Swiss Alps. They are prosperous Mr. and Mrs. Frank Reilly, and Marcia Cram, a New York girl employed in London. Maria is to decide whether she will marry Tim Greenough, who is to join her for Christmas. While awaiting him in the railroad station, Count deHerloczy, a dashing cavalier, flirts boldly with her. At the Waldschloss' gay traditional Noel dinner, Marcia meets the Count formally."

Cleveland's children have done their fair share of seasonal reading as well. Mary Schreiber, Youth Collection Development Specialist at the Cuyahoga County Public Library, has a good vantage point for observing the popular children's Christmas books around Cleveland:

A COOL READ: *The Polar Express* **is a Christmas favorite at local libraries.**

CLASSICALLY CHRISTMAS

Clevelanders are attuned to all types of music, ranging from classical to rock-n-roll and polka. Their taste in classical music is exemplified by looking at some of the best-selling Cleveland Orchestra recordings sold in the Cleveland Orchestra Store during the Christmas season.

1. *A Joyous Celebration* features our organ (with Todd Wilson playing the E.M. Skinner Organ in Severance Hall), and is a consistent favorite.

2. Violinist Lev Polyakin (Cleveland Orchestra Assistant Concertmaster) has a popular CD called *Christmas Kaleidoscope.*

3. Among the things that consistently sell out during the holidays are The Cleveland Orchestra recordings of Beethoven's Symphony No. 9 featuring current and previous conductors: they include George Szell—who made us what we are today, Lorin Maazel, Christoph von Dohnányi, and Franz Welser-Möst.

4. Another great item that sells throughout the season is the Christoph von Dohnányi boxed set, *the Cleveland Orchestra: Christoph von Dohnányi, conductor, Live Performances 1984 through 2001,* a 10-CD set. It's a very diverse collection.

5. *The Robert Shaw Legacy Compact Disc Edition* is a boxed set featuring the Cleveland Orchestra and the Cleveland Orchestra Chorus.

6. Some newer DVDs highlight the Cleveland Orchestra and Severance Hall, both the interior and exterior. They include *Bruckner Symphony No. 7, The Cleveland Orchestra, Franz Welser-Möst, Conductor, Recorded live at Severance Hall, Cleveland, September 25 and 26 , 2008.* Also, Music Director Franz Welser-Möst's live DVD recording, *The Cleveland Orchestra in Performance: Bruckner Symphony No. 8.*

7. Anything by Mitsuko Uchida is very popular. She has been focusing on the Mozart recordings, and she has several CDs (including *The Cleveland Orchestra, Mitsuko Uchida, conductor and piano, Piano Concerto 20 and Piano Concerto 27*)."

—Larry Fox, manager, Cleveland Orchestra Store and Blossom Bandwagon Store

RALPHIE FOR YOUR TREE: The film *A Christmas Story* popularized leg lamps, renewed interest in Red Ryder B.B. guns, and has inspired more than one Christmas ornament.

C'MON OVER TO RALPHIE'S HOUSE: Ralphie's house from *A Christmas Story*, and now *A Christmas Story* House and Museum, on Cleveland's West Side.

The Night Before Christmas has been shared for generations. One of my favorites versions has illustrations by Jan Brett, and when I used it with families at the library, many would have it memorized and would start reading along with me.

Chris Van Allsburg's *The Polar Express* is a library program must in December. Families come dressed in pajamas to be spirited away to the North Pole in a reading of the story, enjoy some Christmas cookies, and receive a bell from Santa. When I hosted a Polar Express night at the North Olmsted Branch in 2010 there were over 100 people in attendance.

Christmas just isn't Christmas without Cindy Lou Who and the Grinch. All Dr. Seuss books have remained popular, but *How the Grinch Stole Christmas* is a must during the holiday season.

If you're looking for a great way to introduce young girls and boys to the *Nutcracker* story before seeing the ballet, check out Mary Engelbreit's exquisite adaptation. Clara, Uncle Drosselmeyer, and the Nutcracker Prince are given new life through her signature artwork. —*Mary Schreiber, Youth Collection Development Specialist, Cuyahoga County Public Library*

A CHRISTMAS STORY, CLEVELAND-STYLE

While the rest of the country is content with glimpses of the past when watching the 1983 now-classic Christmas film, *A Christmas Story*, Clevelanders are on the lookout for views of their city. And they're not disappointed—the Terminal Tower, Public Square, Higbee's inside and out, and "Cleveland Street," a.k.a. West 11th Street are all featured. While portions of *A Christmas Story* were filmed in Toronto, other parts were shot in Cleveland and involved locals as extras and crew.

Based on Jean Shepherd's book, *In God We Trust, All Others Pay Cash*, the movie *A Christmas Story* is set in Hammond, Indiana, where the author grew up. As most Clevelanders know, though, this house in the film is actually on Cleveland's west side

Californian Brian Jones is the owner of A Christmas Story House and Museum in Cleveland. Made famous by the film, the house is located at 3159 West 11th Street, and is now open to visitors who want to recapture some of the nostalgia. According to Cuyahoga County records, the house was built in 1895.

One of many memorable elements of *A Christmas Story* is Ralphie's dream Christmas gift, the official Red Ryder Carbine-Action Two-Hundred-Shot Range-Model Air

Rifle. Brian Jones notes, "Only three of the guns were made for the movie. The author combined the Red Ryder and another gun, so Daisy had to make some specially, with a compass and sundial."

Brian Jones mentions how Higbee's came to be featured in the film. "The directors and producers were looking for a place to film inside a department store. The author was from Hammond, Indiana, and went to his home town, and Marshall Field in Chicago, and finally, Higbee's."

R. Bruce Campbell (1936–2012), the Higbee Company's president of administration, is the one credited with making it possible for portions of *A Christmas Story* to be shot inside Higbee's. "Bruce Campbell of Higbee's was the only one who wanted to take the project on," Brian Jones says. "It was a big project, and they had all the employees as extras. Higbee's had to take down the current merchandise and put up 1940s-style things."

Not all of *A Christmas Story* was shot in Cleveland. "They would have filmed more scenes here if it had been colder. The snow you saw around the house was firefighters' foam and flakes. It was all fake snow," Brian Jones says.

Jim Gelarden, who was an art department production assistant on the film, discusses some of the specifics we all remember, including the Little Orphan Annie secret decoder ring.

ON THE TRAIL OF AN ORPHAN ANNIE SECRET DECODER RING

I got this call from the set decorators to meet with them in the old Stouffer's Hotel, and they talked to me about working on a period movie. They had a list of things they were looking for. They gave me this list of items, some money to buy Polaroid film, and said to go out and find these items and take pictures of them. That's how the whole thing got started.

The list that they gave me included toys—period wind-up toys, radios, perfume bottles, all the displays that were in Higbee's later on. So I spent a few days going around taking Polaroids of all these things, and then when they came to town, I laid them all out on the table, by category. They were amazed that I had found all this stuff, because they didn't think they could find any of it in Cleveland. They thought they'd have to bring it all in from L.A. or Toronto, which is where they were from.

Then they said, 'There is one thing that you can't find.' I said, 'What's that?' They had a picture of an Orphan Annie decoder ring. They were

A DIFFERENT CHRISTMAS STORY: In 1950, *The Cleveland News* ran serialized " Christmas Holiday" fiction by Sarah-Elizabeth Rodger.

"They would have filmed more scenes here if it had been colder."

going to have it made by a prop specialist in Toronto. I said, 'Wait. I know where you can get these.' They said, 'No, you can't. You can't find them." I said, 'What year do you want for the decoder rings? They came in years.' I knew a collector in Cleveland who had a bunch of those. I went out and bought some and brought them in. The Little Orphan Annie decoder rings had a ring of letters and numbers that you could line up to come up with a code, and there would be a secret message, which had to do with Ovaltine.

After that, they gave me cash to start procuring and renting items. They secured a warehouse in the back of Tower City for storage space and we started gathering all the collections of toys and helped find the streetlights that they used. —*Jim Gelarden*

TYING A BOW ON YOUR INTERNSHIP

I interned with The Higbee Company when I went to the Cleveland Institute of Art. As part of my internship, I worked on *A Christmas Story*. I stapled snow, and they said, 'Does anybody know how to make a bow?' I said, 'Yes, I know how to make a bow.' So my claim to fame is that in *A Christmas Story*, there's a scene with a fruit basket and the bow on the fruit basket is mine. The way you'll be able to tell is I cut a tail—it's the signature on all my bows. —*Joe Valenti*

LEG LAMPS AND BEYOND

A Christmas Story was well written enough that it pulled some sort of emotional connection out of every person viewing it. —*Christopher G. Axelrod*

THE TOY OF TOYS FOR A BOY

One reason why the movie *A Christmas Story* is so special is because for that kid, the Red Ryder [Carbine-Action Two Hundred-Shot Range Model Air Rifle] was the toy of toys. You could have given him a car or a motorcycle but that was the one thing he wanted. —*Steve Presser*

GREAT LEG: The leg lamp from *A Christmas Story* has become a classic in its own right.

"Does anybody know how to make a bow?"

Local Traditions

Deck the halls, and walls, and malls: That seemed to be the local motto as Clevelanders prepared for the approach of Christmas. Decorating the city became an event in itself, with community tree-lighting ceremonies and other celebrations. Activities such as Christmas parades were all outdoors, but by the late sixties, more mall-crawlers experienced the season without having to brave the weather. As Christmas drew closer, it was time for annual Christmas parties, caroling and more.

LET THERE BE LIGHTS, AND LOTS OF THEM

Clevelanders have an up-close-and-personal connection to some of the traditions enjoyed by the rest of the country, including Christmas lights. Back in 1923, the first National Christmas Tree was illuminated by lights produced at GE's Nela Park in Cleveland: When President Calvin Coolidge lit that tree, it glowed with twenty-five-hundred red, white, and blue bulbs. Since then, Nela Park, the corporate headquarters of the General Electric Company Incandescent Lamp Division, has continued to design and produce the lights used on the National Christmas Tree in Washington, D.C. Closer to home, locals have flocked to GE's Nela Park on Noble Road in East Cleveland since the 1920s to experience the splendor of the Christmas lighting displays first hand. Until 1959, when the volume of drive-through traffic made it prohibitive, light-gazers could drive through the campus. In 1975, GE's Nela Park was added to the U.S. Department of the Interior National Register of Historic Places.

LIGHT INSPIRATION:
In the 1970s, GE's Nela
Park created Christmas
cards with lights.

MAMA, SANTA, AND MAMA SANTA'S

When I was a single mom with a four-year-old daughter, time was often in short supply relative to those expectations of the Perfect Holiday. Stephanie and I had just moved to Cleveland Heights and I'd vowed repeatedly to take her to see the lights at GE's Nela Park and Public Square. As we grabbed a pizza for dinner one night, she reminded me again that I'd promised we'd see the lights before Santa came. I did the math and realized it was the last night I could make good on my promise. Inside the restaurant—Mama Santa's in Little Italy—we grabbed a couple of Cokes and extra napkins along with our pizza, clambered back in the car, made a left on Euclid Avenue, and zoomed toward downtown. We toured Public Square's luminous winter garden while eating our scrumptious, messy pizza (double cheese and extra sauce) and hit Nela Park on the way up Noble Road hill heading home. The traffic, bumper to bumper, allowed us to feast a long time on the gleaming kaleidoscope of trees, snowmen, toy soldiers and reindeer while we crunched on the last of our 'pizza bones.' For her, this night turned into a strangely hilarious combination of dinner and entertainment and though she is now an adult, she insists we never miss a Christmas touring the lights while eating our Mama Santa's pizza. So far, we've always made good on keeping this annual uniquely Cleveland holiday tradition.
—*Cindy Washabaugh*

DRIVE-THRU MEMORY LANE

Every year my family went to Nela Park. It was the greatest, incredible. Back in the day when we were kids, they allowed you to go through. We didn't have too many Christmas lights in our neighborhood—it was a Jewish neighborhood. To see the Christmas lights at Nela Park was just amazing, the characters that they created and the twinkling. We always went there when there was a little bit of snow. —*Steve Presser*

TREE LIGHTING CEREMONIES AND CHRISTMAS PARADES

Often, the tree-lighting ceremonies around our city drew national celebrities. In 1960, for instance, Johnny Mathis sang at the City of Cleveland's ceremony on November 25th. He sang with the Cleveland Heights High School's A Cappella Choir, and Mayor Celebrezze spoke at the event. At the Shaker Square tree lighting ceremonies, Santa has arrived by various methods over the years, including on an English double-decker bus.

In 1975, the Jackson Five took part in the eighth annual Cleveland Christmas parade when they rode on a float from East 18th Street to Public Square in 31 mph wind gusts. That day, it was a chilly thirty-three degrees. The parade was co-sponsored by radio station WIXY and the May Company, with eighty-six different organizations with bands, floats and trucks. One spokesperson estimated the parade attendance at 100,000, and *The Plain Dealer* reported that by the time the Jackson Five's float got to Public Square, it was being pursued by a mob that trampled snow fences and overwhelmed auxiliary police.

Larry Morrow discusses his role as emcee for Cleveland's Christmas tree

PAWS IN THE PARADE:
Floats were part of the
Cleveland Press Christmas
Parade spectacle in 1964.

SPECTATOR SPORT:
Watching the Cleveland
Christmas Parade was a
favorite activity.

lighting ceremonies and taking part in Cleveland's Christmas parade for thirty-four years. Given the honorary title of "Mr. Cleveland" by former mayor George Voinovich, Larry Morrow's four decades on the radio in Cleveland began in 1966 at WIXY 1260:

> My holiday schedule started on Thanksgiving Day; I'd be on the air. Friday night was the Christmas tree lighting ceremony. Saturday was the parade downtown. So those three days in a row, at times, would absolutely wipe me out. But it was wonderful exposure and I loved every minute of it. Christmas has always been a very big part of my life.
>
> At the Friday Christmas tree lighting ceremony, I was the emcee for many years. I can remember back when I was at WIXY, as the emcee for that event. We would have, maybe, a couple thousand people who would show up for it on Friday evening. The mayor would be there, and Santa Claus would turn on the lights.
>
> I arrived at WIXY in 1966, about 6 months after the station went on the air, and in 1967 we had the very first WIXY-May Company Christmas Parade. At that time, WIXY's ratings were beginning to really bulge and all of a sudden we were number one in town. Our very first parade in 1967 was a huge success. We had over 100,000 people there.
>
> That parade continued all the years that I was at WIXY. When I went to 3WE (WWWE) the Christmas parade continued, and that's when I started to ride in the parade with Mr. Jingeling, Halle's wonderful Keeper of the Keys. Then, as I went to Q104 (WQAL), we sponsored the parade as well, and I continued to ride in the parade with Mr. Jingeling. We had our own float. I have such wonderful remembrances of those days. I was in parades at WIXY, all of my ten years at 3WE (WWWE), and then the fifteen years at WQAL; I was in every one of those parades.
>
> David Cassidy was a huge star in the sixties, and I believe we had him in 1968 or 1969, when he had the hit television show and hit records. When WIXY brought him in, it sort of brought the house down. The kids were lined up all the way down Euclid Avenue— from East 20th Street all the way down to the Square—screaming when he came by in his float. —*Larry Morrow, author of* This is Larry Morrow . . . My Life On and Off the Air

HOW WE LOVED A PARADE

They had a Christmas parade downtown. As our girls grew, we would dress them up, and our neighbor and her family joined us as we headed downtown. We got a hotel room at Public Square for

WAVES OF EXCITEMENT: Santa arrives in the 1964 *Cleveland Press* **Christmas Parade.**

the day. The kids would be all dressed up in the highest of fashions, and in a bag was their winter attire for the parade. We'd check into the hotel, hang the dresses and suit jackets carefully so as not to wrinkle them, and bundle the kids up to sit in the cold to watch the parade down on the Square. How they loved a parade, and this Christmas parade did not disappoint them. Following the parade, we rushed back to the hotel, warmed up, got dressed up beautifully again, and ventured out for the familiar day of seeing Santa and all the other spectacular sights of the season. . . . Times were good, life was fun, and the spirit of Christmas was alive and well. That was a very warm, wonderful feeling. —*Patricia Harrison*

COOL PARADE

At the parade downtown, I remember being cold and not being able to see, waiting for Santa Claus. —*Bunny Sullivan Trepal*

NATIVITY SCENES AROUND THE CITY

At Cleveland churches and elsewhere, Nativity scenes were part of the Christmas commemoration. Some were more elaborate than others, including life-sized mangers.

COME ONE, COME ALL: *Cleveland Press* banners led the way, followed by floats, marching bands, and of course, Santa.

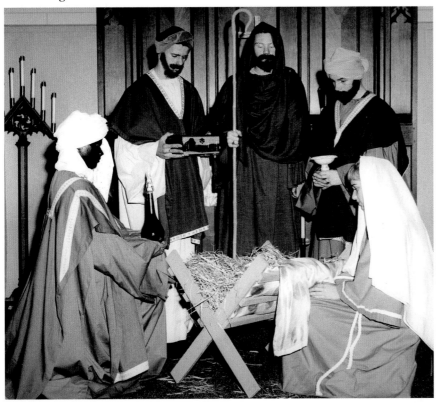

NATIVITY SCENE, SOUTH EUCLID: 1959, St. John Lutheran Church.

PUTTING UP THE MANGER

As a kid, I attended Immaculate Heart of Mary on Lansing Avenue in Cleveland. As a teenager I started helping the nuns put up the life-sized manger in the church. After a few years of being their helper, they were happy to hand the job over to me. They were always around to check up on my progress. They were nearby, decorating the main altar and other parts of the church.

The custodian delivered the six or seven Christmas trees and I placed them around the stable. Many years before, the nuns had made this fake 'rock' for the manger scene that was made with earth-toned paint on canvas that can be crushed to look like the rocky hills of Bethlehem. That was placed at the base, and the statues were pretty big and were placed around the manger. Working in such a grand church like that certainly got you in the Christmas spirit! Usually, at midnight Mass, church was always darkened except for candles and lights around the manger. A young school child brought in the Baby Jesus and put the statue in the manger. I was always told, 'Make sure there's access!' when setting up the manger scene so the child could get through the display and put the statue easily in the stable.

Then the priest blessed the manger, the lights would come on, and people would sing.

After I got my manger 'chops' at Immaculate Heart, I began helping out at the Franciscan-run Church of St. Stanislaus (on East 65th Street in Slavic Village), and began assembling their new life-sized manger. The manger is a colossal structure that takes up the entire west transept of an equally colossal Gothic church. To give it height for all people to see, we actually put tables on top of tables, and then put the twelve-foot-tall Christmas trees on them, behind the stable, and assembled all of the other trees around it. Each year Heritage Farms in Peninsula, Ohio, donated the Christmas trees—ten to fifteen, some as big as twelve feet, that we would pick up with trucks that parishioners donated. When I took on this gigantic task at St. Stanislaus, I had helpers—some 8th grade boys. Each year, as the boys progressed through high school and then college, they continued to look forward to helping out. We called ourselves the Major Manger Managers and we worked together for three evenings before Christmas and had a great time assembling the trees, lights, and statues. It is truly a memory now since a few years ago, with other domestic

MEMORABLE MANGER SCENE: Nativity scene at the Church of the Immaculate Heart of Mary, Cleveland, circa 1980.

SINGING IN THE HOLIDAYS: Christmas carols were part of the 1961 Italian Cultural Garden Association's Yultide party.

CHRISTMAS EVE OR CHRISTMAS MORNING: Family traditions varied as to when to open gifts.

tasks to take care of at home, I chose to give up my direction of the manger operation. Now those same eighth-grade boys—all grown up and some with families and kids of their own—continue to be the Major Manger Managers.
—*Richard Konisiewicz*

CAROLING

For some, music was part of the celebration of Christmas—singing carols in the neighborhoods of Cleveland and its suburbs and playing music in private homes.

NEIGHBORHOOD CAROLING PARTY

The caroling party in Bratenahl began around 1963 at Rita and Stanley Roediger's house. They invited the community and had a violinist who played in the Cleveland Orchestra; Rita played the piano. That tradition continued throughout the sixties. They invited everybody in the community. Mary, Mary (Mary Strassmeyer) wrote about it in her column. I think it ended right before we got here, in 1985. Later the P.T.A. took it over until the school closed, and then the Bratenahl Community Foundation. Today the tradition continues, with parties held at different people's houses.
—*Chris Spano*

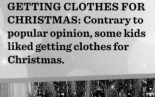

GETTING CLOTHES FOR CHRISTMAS: Contrary to popular opinion, some kids liked getting clothes for Christmas.

POCKETS FULL OF SILVER

My sister and I played violin as children—and still do. Every Christmas we had a command performance for my father's parents in front of their Christmas tree on Cannon Avenue in Lakewood. My grandfather was the cantor at St. Mary's Romanian Orthodox Church for fifty years, so there was no fudging on pitch or tempo. We played through traditional Romanian Christmas carols like "O Ce Veste" in perfect two-part precision and were always joined by my father and grandfather belting out the chorus in flawless harmony. Afterward, my grandfather would reward us with pockets full of silver coins (the kind that predated those with nasty copper centers) that were mostly half dollars and silver dollars. —*George Ghetia*

PIZZA AND HARMONY

The best pizza I ever had was at Tony's at Kamm's. I grew up in St. Mel's Parish. To get more money to get pizza at Tony's, we'd go Christmas caroling door-to-door, saying we were from the St. Mel's Athletic Fund. It was an early entrepreneurial bait-and-switch adventure. We were from St. Mel's, we were athletes, and we did have a fund—to get money to feed ourselves at Tony's. A lot of people would give us a dollar. In 1957, that was a lot for four kids singing. We were pretty good singers. We were all in the choir—and we were all fast. We did one song, and got out.

I can't remember exactly when we did this, since it couldn't have been Christmas Eve. But it seemed that most homes had small gatherings going, or maybe they just had big families, and it was during the Christmas season. Every house knew the drill: Somebody shows up on your porch and jumps into a Christmas carol, and you give them money.

This took place in the outer fringes of West Park, an area bounded on the north by Lakewood Heights Boulevard (later wiped out by I-90) and on the west by Warren Road. —*Bob Krummert*

CHRISTMAS WITH HOPE

Baby Boomers grew up watching Bob Hope Christmas specials on television. When he was four years old, Bob Hope (born Leslie Townes Hope) moved with his family to Cleveland from England and grew up here. He attended Cleveland's East High School. The first Bob Hope Christmas special aired in 1953.

I remember listening to the Cleveland radio stations wear out 'Jingle Bell Rock,' 'Rockin' Around the Christmas Tree,' and 'Blue Christmas' during the holidays. Also, the Bob Hope Christmas Specials on television. —*Paul Negulescu*

THE BOAR'S HEAD AND YULE LOG FESTIVAL

In 1961, the Boar's Head and Yule Log Festival made its debut at Trinity Cathedral, Cleveland, when Episcopal Bishop Nelson M. Burroughs brought the tradition from Christ Church Cathedral, Cincinnati. Originally it was a Christmas celebration funded by the Episcopal Diocese of Ohio, and although that is no longer the case, the event continues and is still held yearly at Trinity Cathedral. For fifty years, Clevelanders have had the opportunity to participate in this Elizabethan Christmas experience, rich with pageantry, music, and hints of old English Christmas celebrations. Drawing on traditions, some of which date back to the Middle Ages, the Boar's Head Festival is filled with symbols such as a boar's head, (representing the triumph of good over evil), and a yule log, which was traditionally burned in English manor houses at Christmastime.

Cindy Wyszynski, current chairperson of the Boar's Head and Yule Log Festival Committee, and Hans VanWormer, director of the festival, are part of a team of thirteen who work to continue this local Christmas tradition. Cindy discusses a few of the details of earlier festivals: "The Boar's Head Festival was commonly held between the Christmas and New Year's holidays. The original Boar's Head costumes in 1960 were handmade by Episcopal Women's Guilds around the diocese, but there were no women *in* the festival until 1978 . . . We have two boar's heads; the one most frequently seen was freeze-dried to preserve it, and it is presented on a platter surrounded by greens, fruits, and red ribbons and carried in a processional. The yule log is probably four or five feet long and is secured to its own wagon, which is pulled and pushed by a group of costumed children (the 'woodsmen'), while one of them rides on the log."

Music is a major part of the Boar's Head and Yule Log Festival, the original score having evolved over the years. The pageant features music associated with costumed actors in the Nativity story, such as Mary and Joseph, the Three Kings, shepherds (with sheep), as well as King Wenceslas. There are the Beefeaters, (yeomen of the British monarch's Royal Guard), dancing peasants, and group singers such as the Ladies of the Court. "We have costumes for twenty Beefeaters in the festival every year," Cindy Wyszynski says. "Their original costumes were made in 1960, and have just recently been completely remade, at considerable cost. Each year, we accept offerings and donations during the festival presentations. Costume replacement, then, is dependent on those donations."

In addition to sights and sounds, the Boar's Head Festival has always included aromas of frankincense, freshly baked mince pie, and ham. "There is no 'feast' attached to the Festival," Cindy Wyszynski explains, "but after the second presentation, the attendees are invited to join the cast and crew in eating the food carried in the procession. That includes the three-foot mince pies—with fruit, nuts, rum, and a homemade crust—baked by a committee member in a large pizza oven—as well as plum pudding and ham."

GREETING CARDS

Speaking of old traditions, sending and receiving Christmas cards is said to have originated in England in the 1840s. Clevelanders know that many of the cards sent and received around the country were created locally at American Greetings Corporation.

GREETING CARD DÉCOR

My dad used to decorate with greeting cards. We would string them around the ceiling, and he would put tinsel on them and maybe a few bulbs. *—Josephine Kovach*

HOMEMADE CARDS

We made our own potato-print Christmas cards and wrapping paper. We cut a potato in half, took a bell-shaped cookie-cutter, pressed it an inch into a potato, and then cut around it. *—Bunny Sullivan Trepal*

SENDING AND RECEIVING

I remember helping my mom send out Christmas cards—she would send out a ton of them—and receiving Christmas cards from relatives in Romania. The foreign stamps were as interesting as the cards. *—Paul Negulescu*

PARTY TIME

Just before Christmas, downtown restaurants and hotels were booked with a succession of office parties.

When I worked for a law firm in the early 1980s our Christmas party was held at the Hollenden House. The Champagne flowed and everyone dressed up. The office closed early and we all headed over to the hotel. People were gracious, and there were no boundaries between the partners, associates and staff. Everyone mingled. I had never been to anything that glamorous. *—Pat Fernberg*

BIG AS LIFE: Dolls were always at the top of the list for Christmas gifts.

CHRISTMAS EVE IN CLEVELAND HOMES

We all know the line about the night before Christmas when all through house, not a creature was stirring. . . . However, it seems that on Christmas Eve, you didn't find many Cleveland households to fit that description.

A BABY IS BORN

Midnight Mass was always special, but one year my mom went into labor with my brother Corky while my dad and grandma were at Mass. One of the neighbors went to get my dad so he could take my mom to Lakewood Hospital. Corky was the best present that year. —*Helen Wirt*

THE JOY OF CHRISTMAS: Decorations, gifts, and togetherness.

A STORY IS RETOLD

Before our open house guests arrived on Christmas Eve, the immediate family always gathered in the living room, where my father read the Bible story of the birth of Jesus from the book of Luke. I was always impressed that he knew just which page to turn to, and found it touching. The rest of Christmas Eve, except for when the carolers came, was devoted to the big party with lots of hoopla and expensive food and drink. Then, before bedtime on Christmas Eve, one of our parents would read *The Night Before Christmas*, and we were allowed to open one gift each. It was always the same thing: scratchy Christmas pajamas that we were supposed to wear to bed. —*Laurie Orr*

THE SCENE IS SET

In my family, the tradition was that Santa brought the tree on Christmas Eve. My parents served oyster stew, got cookies for Santa, set out a cup of cocoa by the armchair near the fireplace, and put us to bed. My dad would go out and get a tree; lots of places were closed. They would decorate the tree, wrap presents, and set up the Nativity scene on the baby grand piano. They'd go to bed at 3:00 a.m., and we got up at 4:00 a.m. They'd say, 'Get back in bed.' For us kids, it was really magical. the magic of coming downstairs and seeing it all. —*Katie Daley*

BIG CHRISTMAS MEMORIES

Members of big families have big memories of Christmas morning: There were lots of kids, lots of wrapping paper, and lots of memories in the making.

THE TREE IS TRIMMED

We usually trimmed our tree on Christmas Eve. The closer you got to December 25th, the better deal you got on a tree. One year we picked up a decent tree just after dinner for only two bucks. My father quickly trimmed the bottom of the trunk, screwed it into a cast-iron base, and we had it lit and decorated with hours to spare before Santa's arrival. —*Joe Valencic*

SANTA IS SIGHTED

I remember listening to the television news as a child on Christmas Eve, when the weatherman or anchorman would announce a Santa sighting. Santa was usually seen in Norway or China. Looking back, it was something to hear the anchorman say, 'Santa has been spotted in France, and one of the airports has reported seeing a red nose on one of his reindeer.' —*Pat Fernberg*

THE CELEBRATION BEGINS

I grew up on Tillman Avenue, around West 52nd and Detroit. I have an Italian heritage, and our whole Christmas was a celebration, usually in two days. We would have a party down in the basement when we'd all get together on Christmas Eve. We had homemade Italian sausage, homemade wine, homemade pizza. We had a lot of people over, with music and drinking, and festivity. We'd open our gifts on Christmas Eve. It was more of a celebration for us than Christmas morning. At twelve o'clock we would go to St. Stephen's Church, a beautiful church. We'd come back after church and eat a little more. —*Josephine Kovach*

PRESENT OPENING AS THEATER: Kids opened their gifts while adults looked on.

MEMORIES OF CHRISTMAS DAY

On Christmas morning, just about every kid in the city was an early riser, maybe even as early as 4:00 a.m. Some were wearing their new Christmas pajamas. Trees were lit, lovingly wrapped presents were ready to be opened, and Santa left evidence of his visits: cookie crumbs and half-consumed glasses of milk or cups of cocoa in living rooms across the city.

**HANG 'EM HIGH: For kids, Christmas Eve kindled
high-caliber excitement.**

ALWAYS USE A TRIPOD

My mother was being driven crazy by her five young children while preparing for our annual Christmas Eve party when the phone rang. "Jeannie, it's Perry," the gruff voice said. I was seven years old, and I could hear his voice over the phone as Perry Cragg, the chief photographer for the Cleveland News, made his pitch. "I'm on deadline to get a heart-warming Christmas photo for the paper. Could I come over right now and take a picture of your kids in front of the fireplace in their pajamas, looking like they're waiting for Santa?"

The subtext was that he and my father, who was a newspaper reporter, were friends. Perry Cragg hung up before my mother could say she was too busy. He showed up with the press camera of the day, a 4x5 Speed Graphic, and a tripod. I was already interested in all things newsy and visual, so I watched with rapt attention as he lined up my brother and sister in front of the fireplace. My mother wanted my brother John to take off his gun belt, but Perry Cragg thought it added a nice touch. He even had my brother aim his pistol at the fireplace. My sister Nicole was told to reach for a stocking. To get the right angle, Perry Cragg had to set the camera on a tripod on the steps going to our second floor. "Kid," he said, "the young photographers always make fun of me for using a tripod. If you want a sharp negative, always use a tripod. Don't forget that." It was a heavy message for a seven-year-old two days before Christmas.

—*Stephen P. Bellamy*

'TIS THE SEASON

After all the holiday stories I have done through the years, I still believe that one of the best places to get a holiday boost is in the restored canal town of Roscoe Village in Coshocton.

They begin the season with an outdoor candle-lighting ceremony about the first weekend in December. I was invited one year to be the "official candle lighter," and I arrived on a very cold and dark December night. The town looked like a page from a Dickens novel, with frost painting the edges of windows. Guides from the village's various attractions were dressed in nineteenth-century frock coats or hoop skirts. Street-lights from another era illuminated the walks and roadways, where thousands of people milled about, waiting for the ceremony to begin.

A brass ensemble wandered the streets playing Christmas carols, while small groups of carolers strolled in front of the stores, singing the songs of the season.

My duties were simple. I was given a brief introduction to polite applause, and as I stepped forward to the podium, the lights along the streets went out. I struck a match and lit a candle I was holding. For a moment, as I wished the crowd a Merry Christmas, I held in my hand the only light on the street. In the darkness, several thousand people stood crowded around the stage. The flickering light from my candle reflected on the faces around the edge of the stage.

(continues on next page)

A HAIR-CURLING DAY

I had poker-straight hair as a child, and wished I had curly hair like my mom and sisters. So on Christmas Eve, my mom would curl my hair using rag rollers—basically strips of cloth she would tear from old clothes in the rag bag to curl my hair. In Christmas morning pictures, I would be in my robe under the Christmas tree with my hair still in the rag rollers. But later in the day, I would have lovely curls for Christmas. —*Kathie Brown*

A HOT TIME

On Christmas morning, we'd have to be on the second floor—you couldn't come down—lined up, youngest to oldest, in our pajamas or robe. My mother would be at the bottom of the stairs; she had the movie camera and my father was holding the extension cord. She'd call our names, and one by one, we had to come down the stairs looking into the camera with amazement on our faces. There was no audio, of course. Then off you would go, scurrying to the Christmas tree while she captured the next child coming down. When you were really little, you came down the stairs in reverse, as a child crawling. The older kids, or at least the teens, walked down with coolness.

My mother was a former top model, a beautiful, beautiful woman who always had her hair done, well-coiffed. Her hair was immaculate for the holidays, as always. The fashion of the day was to have very sculpted hair, with lots of setting solution and hairspray.

AFTER A BIG DAY: The excitement of Christmas could be exhausting.

"Her hair was immaculate for the holidays, as always."

Those movie cameras needed movie lights, and they had big light bars with about four to six huge, hot floodlights with no protection on them whatsoever. You held the handle in one hand and the movie camera in the other, with six extremely hot lights over your head generating light for the film. My mother called the first child, who came down the stairs, and the next child came down and said, 'Mom! Mom!' She wanted to get this done, and wouldn't acknowledge us saying, 'But, Mom!'

The floodlights were too close to her hair, and her hair had caught fire. She dropped the camera, dropped the lights, and ran for the kitchen sink. She was fine, but she had some singed hair on the top that had to be cut out and rebalanced. —*Christopher G. Axelrod*

LET IT SNOW

One Christmas in the 1950s, everything was snowbound and you had to dig out. The city was absolutely paralyzed and it kept snowing and snowing. It was fascinating to see the snow up above the window ledges. What an adventure that was! It was like being in the Arctic, but it was fun to be at home with your gifts, knowing that you were safe and that there was still power and everything. —*Dennis Gaughan*

(continued)

I walked across the stage and, leaning towards the crowd, started to light other candles held by their outstretched hands. The light spread outward from my candle and, in moments, pinpoints of light climbed the hill behind me and ignited a river of candles in the street on both sides of me. I led the crowd in singing "Silent Night." Never before had the song seemed so real and so personal as it did on this magical night in Roscoe Village, where I stood bathed in the light of thousands of candles. —*Neil Zurcher, from his book* Tales From the Road

THIS JUST IN: CHRISTMAS-TIME NEWS FLASHES FROM THE PAST

In his online "Calendar of Cleveland Dismalia," author John Stark Bellamy II offers a day-by-day account of news headlines from Cleveland's past. He is the author of six books and two anthologies about local crimes and disasters. Here are a few of his examples of "Forest City Woe" that took place at Christmas:

DECEMBER 24

- The Cleveland Heights police apprehend would-be safecrackers at St. Paul's Episcopal Church at Coventry Rd. and Fairmount Blvd. (1925)

- Robbers get away with $3,000 in a heist at the Washington Federal Savings & Loan Co. at Shaker Square. (1966)

- Milton Battle's delicatessen at 8632 Buckeye Rd. is robbed for the 38th time in 27 years; Battle vows to continue his business there. (1980)

- No one is hurt as a Convair 640 turbo jet freight plane crashes at Cleveland Hopkins Airport. (1983)

(Continues on next page)

A NEW FAMILY TRADITION

In 1969 or 1970, influenced by popular philosophies of the late sixties, we drew names out of a hat, one person's name each. We each gave that person a gift. There was no wrapping paper, we used newspaper, and you had to make the present. We decorated our tree with strings of popcorn and cranberries that we sewed together piece by piece. It was easy—you didn't have to be a seamstress to do it. It was kind of soothing to sit around and talk; we were storytellers. I think it was an effort on my parents' part to pull us all together when we were teenagers. It was the most memorable Christmas to me, out of any in my life. We did that for a few years. My oldest brother, Bill, made a rope ladder that I still have. It's five feet high, with each step painted differently. —*Katie Daley*

DISHING UP A GREAT GIFT

In 1970, early Christmas morning I found in my stocking the usual things: fruit, candy, socks, personal hygiene stuff, and a small roll of paper with a red ribbon tied into a bow around it. The paper looked like it came from the phone message pad. I looked over at my mom as I started to untie the ribbon and the smile on her face started me thinking, 'Something is up.'

In our house, Christmas morning is a mad rush to tear and destroy wrapping paper and eat candy at 6:30 a.m. My family is made up of eight children and we all are going nuts like a tornado in our living room. As I was untying the ribbon I looked across the room again and my mother had a wide smile and tears in her eyes. Our eyes meet and time stopped. I unrolled the paper and in her wonderful printing were the words 'No more dishes for you . . . Merry Christmas . . . 1970!'

For me, time stopped. Our eyes met again, we smiled, I yelled, and the room went silent. I quickly stood up and walked over piles of wrapping paper and gifts, gave my mother a huge hug and kiss, and thanked her for the best Christmas present ever. In our house doing the dishes was a huge task. Kitchen duty lasted seven days and we rotated based on age and ability. It involved food prep, setting the table for ten—then clean-up for ten—and no dishwasher. Clean-up was the worst: plates, glasses, silverware and pots and pans. It took forever! I was seventeen in 1970, and had been doing the dishes since I could reach the sink, and this Christmas morning it came to an end. My best present ever! —*Jon Thibo*

TREE TOTS

I remember as a child our Christmas tree was always in a bottomless play pen to keep that year's toddler from pulling the tree down. The tree was also tied to the curtain rod for safe measure. —*Helen Wirt*

A CHRISTMAS FIT FOR THE ELEVEN KINGS

Preparations for Christmas began about three weeks before, when Aunt Esther came over to decorate the house. With the help of us kids she still managed to get the decorations up in one day. Mom had shopping down to a science and would get her shopping done in as few trips as possible. She had the majority of the gifts delivered to one our neighbors to keep them away from our snooping eyes.

On Christmas Eve, after all the children were nestled in their beds, Santa would come. The first thing he did was decorate our Christmas tree. Mom and Dad could not bear the thought of us 'helping' them decorate the tree. The gifts from Santa, the unwrapped gifts, were placed in individual piles along with wrapped gifts from Mom and Dad. Somehow, we always knew which pile was ours.

When Christmas morning finally arrived, sometimes as early as 5:00 a.m., we would wake up Mom and Dad. We would all gather around the basement steps and have to wait until R.J. (Dad) went downstairs to make sure that Santa had come. After what seemed like an hour he would come up and give us permission to go downstairs. This is where the pandemonium occurred: the wrapping paper flying, along with the delighted screams of 'just what I wanted.' Even if we didn't get a particular item we wanted, the gifts always seemed just right. One year, everyone who could ride a bike got a new bike. We later learned that all the bikes had been delivered to the neighbors unassembled. Christmas Eve was a late one for Dad as he had to assemble seven or eight bikes.

We always stayed home on Christmas Day, except to go to Mass. It was great because we got to play with our new games and toys. Grandma and Grandpa Carmody always came over for breakfast. Grandpa would arrive with a huge platter of his homemade cinnamon rolls, which we all loved. Grandma and Grandpa's gift to us was always new pajamas. The boys got pajama sets and the girls got nightgowns. Grandma made them from the softest flannel and they were extra warm on a cold winter nights. Before dinner everyone had to straighten up their pile of gifts and toys. Grandma and Grandpa King would come over for dinner. Their gift was always a brand-new crisp dollar bill under our dinner plates.

As we got older the high school kids would go to midnight Mass and bring home their friends for a late night breakfast. The rule was that

(Continued)

DECEMBER 25

- A powerful winter blizzard brings Cleveland to a halt, shutting down streetcars and railroad service. (1909)

- Two boys playing in the Fullerton Elementary School yard at Fullerton Ave. and East 57th St. discover a newborn baby girl under a portable building on the grounds. The girl has been wrapped in newspaper and left to die, but the boys save her and take her to St. Ann's Hospital. (1927)

- The Calvary Reformed Church at 1920 West 65th St. is swept by fire. (1969)

- A group of duck hunters is rescued off the breakwall at East 9th St. after their boat smashes into the breakwall and sinks. (1979)

In 1961 Delta Records of Ohio released an LP featuring Christmas classics performed by sixteen regional high school choral groups. Part of the proceeds went to fund activities for the Society for Crippled Children.

KINGS FOR A DAY: The King family's Christmas traditions included delighted screams and flying wrapping paper.

everyone had to be gone before the little kids got up for Santa. Many years, it was a close call.

As adults, we started the tradition of picking names for a gift exchange. The youngest person got to give the first gift. The person receiving the gift had to sit in the center of the room and open it. Everyone would ooh and aah over the gift before we could move on to the next gift. By the time all of us were married it could take hours just to do the gift exchange. Mom still insisted that she buy each of her children, their spouses, and their children a gift. She discovered the wonderful world of catalog shopping. She also would come up with themes for each person. This resulted in some pretty unique gifts. Sometimes she liked your theme so much that she would buy the same gift two or three times. Who could blame her? She bought over fifty gifts at Christmas.

We also started a charity tradition. A basket was placed on a table and everyone, including the children, would throw in whatever amount of money they wanted, along with the name of their favorite charity. One charity was drawn from the basket and all the money was donated to that charity. Some very generous gifts have been made by the R.J. King family. —*Tom King, Tim King, Ronnie King Whalen, Gerry King, Peggy King-Neumann, Dennis King, Brian King, Kevin King, Noreen King Hone, Rhea King Wightman, David King*

THE YEAR CHRISTMAS WAS FINALLY 'HEAR'

Not everybody has the day off for Christmas or Christmas Eve. Larry Morrow is one of those with experience working on Christmas. His years on the radio in Cleveland began in 1966 and spanned four decades at WIXY 1260, 3WE (WWWE), WERE, and WQAL. Here's how he spent Christmas 1973:

When I married my darling wife, Rosary, in 1973, we were in our brand-new home in Shaker Heights. Because I talked a lot about my new family and had three young girls at the time, a producer at the radio station said, 'Larry, wouldn't it be great if you woke up on Christmas morning and we did the show from your living room? You, know, right next to the Christmas tree. You could talk about how you guys are going to celebrate your very first Christmas together.' It was the first time that WWWE had done a Christmas show outside of the radio station, and it happened to be in my home. It was really wonderful.

We had very special people in town, and some of the athletes came by. Buddy Bell was there, and Duane Kuiper, and some of the other people I had gotten to know dropped by that morning. The mayor dropped by—not only the mayor of Cleveland, but also the mayor of Shaker Heights. When people dropped by, I would interview them. And of course, I interviewed several people by phone. It had a wonderful kind of holiday feeling. We talked about how we celebrated Christmas and then, of course, the guests I had on talked also about how they celebrated Christmas. I believe we did that for two or three years.

Rosary did what we usually did on Christmas morning. She made pancakes and sausage, and we had eggnog for those who came by. I remember the kids made popcorn balls with honey on them. It was terrific. On Christmas, every once in awhile, they'll reflect on that very first Christmas when we lived in Shaker Heights, with me being on the air and them walking down in their pajamas in the morning. I believe the twins wore the same color pajamas.

Some of the kids opened their gifts on the air. . . . There was so much going on. There were neighbors walking into the house. It was all over our radio station—we promoted the living daylights out of it, and so did the newspapers. People would drive by our home on Byron Road and wonder what was going on. All three TV stations covered it. So you can imagine what my living room looked like on Christmas 1973. —*Larry Morrow*

MERRY MEDICAL CHRISTMAS

When I was working as a nurse, I always volunteered to work holidays, including Christmas, so that people who had kids could be home with their families. Our own family would adjust the time we got together and altered our traditions to accommodate my work schedule. I mostly worked in the emergency room, and everybody tried to keep things upbeat. The patient load was about the same as any other day. There seemed to be more heart attacks, or people who over-ate and *thought* they were having a heart attack. For inpatients at Lakewood Hospital, they would fancy it up: serve holiday things like roast beef and use Christmas napkins on the patient's dinner trays. —*Laurie Orr*

MERRY MEDIA CHRISTMAS

It was always a little unfortunate working on Christmas because you'd be away from you family at key times, but I tried to look at it in a positive light. You got to play a role, maybe a small one, in people's lives on an important

LITTLE DRUMMER BOY: The makings of an offbeat Christmas morning in the 1950s. How long before those drumsticks get "lost"?

SHAKER SQUARE

I grew up in Bellevue, Ohio, about seventy-five miles west of Cleveland. Cleveland had always been my Big Apple. Each year, my mother and father would bring me and my sister here at Christmas to see the sights and do some shopping. One year on the way home, we got almost to Public Square heading west. I said, 'Oh, I didn't see Shaker Square! All my friends got to see Shaker Square, and I didn't get to see it.' My father, who didn't like driving in the city—I can still see him in the midst of all that heavy traffic in downtown Cleveland—made a big U-turn right on Euclid and said, 'I'll show my son Shaker Square.'

To this day, that flash of the myriad lights that the Square was decorated in is imprinted in my brain. I can just pull it up and see what it was like. I was dazzled. I said, 'Oh, I never saw anything so beautiful in my life!'

They had reindeer coming across the top. They had the arrival of Santa Claus, coming in an antique wagon like a carriage. There was romance to it. The lighting was everywhere. It was just intense. They had angels that lit up . . . It wasn't just trees. There was excitement to it. My eyes popped out of my head. It was that wonderful. I mean, it was magic.

I just never dreamed that, number one, I'd be living at Shaker Square and, number two, that I'd have a store at Shaker Square.

—*Dickie Gildenmeister*

day. In radio, when I worked at WKSU, it wasn't that hard; usually there's something special going on so it feels Christmasy. —*Bob Burford*

WORKING ON CHRISTMAS EVE

In the early years of my career I was the junior man in the WJW-TV newsroom and worked many a Christmas Eve and Christmas Day.

One that has stuck in my mind over the years was a Christmas Eve back in the early 1970s. TV 8 news photographer Peter Miller and I were returning to the station from an assignment on East 55th Street late in the night on a picture-postcard, snowy Christmas Eve.

It was one of those brief sightings everyone makes while traveling city streets after dark. Flashes, like lightening, of people, ordinary people, acting out scenes from their lives. In this case it was an obvious family dilemma being played out on a snow-covered sidewalk of Cleveland.

What caught my eye first was a young girl, perhaps seven or eight years old, sobbing uncontrollably while clutching a stuffed animal as a middle-aged woman, presumably her mother, was hitting a tall man, who stood there with his head bowed, stoically taking the abuse, making no effort to defend himself.

It was a sad family tableau surrounded on the sidewalk by a couple of old beat-up easy chairs, a lamp, and several boxes that perhaps had their other belongings stuffed inside.

It was only seconds and we were past them. I wondered out loud to Peter, who was driving, what type of a landlord would evict a family from their apartment on a snowy Christmas Eve. Also, what about the obvious anger of the woman at the man. Had he somehow wasted or misspent the rent payment?

The scene kept bothering us as we reached the lakefront and the road to the television station. Our shift would be ending soon and we would be heading home to spend what was left of Christmas Eve with our own families. But the sight of that little crying girl still troubled us.

"How much cash do you have on you?" Peter suddenly asked as he slowed the car.

"About ten bucks. How about you?" I replied.

We both were thinking the same thing. Between us we had thirty dollars. Peter turned the car around and we started back to see if we could help make the homeless family's night a bit better.

But when we arrived at the storefront site near Euclid Avenue, much to our surprise, there was no sign of the family. Even most of their belongings were gone. Only one trashed easy chair and a couple of boxes were still sitting there wearing a dusting of new-fallen snow.

To this day I have no idea of who the family was or what happened to them. But every time I pass that area of East 55th Street and Euclid Avenue I think of that Christmas Eve and a little girl standing in the snow, crying and clinging to her stuffed animal. —*Neil Zurcher*

THE LAST STAND

We should have known. My husband and son were having a hard time carrying the tree from where they cut it to where it was going to be bound. Then we had a hard time putting it in the stand. Then we realized it was the heaviest tree that we had ever had. The tree was as tall as our living room ceiling, about ten feet tall, and heavy.

On Christmas morning, we were all in the kitchen when we heard a 'whoomph!' We went into the living room, and there was the tree, lying the full length of the living room. I didn't believe it: The whole family was going to be here in an hour, and the tree lay all over the room. My kids said, 'It's okay, Mom. We can pick it up and attach it to the door.' Five minutes later, we heard, 'whoomph!'

I said, "That's it. Get the ornaments off. Get the lights off. We're having company in an hour. Get it out there on the curb." So at nine o'clock on Christmas morning, our tree was out on the curb. People were walking by, probably thinking, 'They have it out here already? What is it with these people?' The kids were looking out at the tree, and said, 'Mom, maybe we could cut it in half.' I said, 'Fine. If you want to handle it, handle it. I'm fixing the meal.' So they cut the top of the tree off and put it back in the stand. We had a five-foot tree. —*Virginia Meil*

FAMILY CELEBRATION:
A souvenir fez from Turkey
was a noteworthy gift.

TAKING A BOUGH: Tree-trimming was a family project.

CUT YOUR OWN
CHRISTMAS TREE
Families Find It FUN!

NEW LYME — ROCK CREEK

THE C H MANNERS CHRISTMAS TREE FARM

KE.1·3717

FOR DO-IT-YOURSELFERS: Cutting your own Christmas tree from a Christmas tree farm.

WITH ALL THE TRIMMINGS

Trees and Decorations at Home

CHRISTMAS TREES: BOUGH WOW

Christmas tree memories tend to fall into two categories: trees for public spaces and trees for private places, like homes. Perhaps Cleveland's most famous trees were the majestic ones holding court year after year in the Sterling-Lindner department store. Other noteworthy trees loomed large in the lobby of the Terminal Tower just outside the door to Higbee's or stood in the public spaces of area malls and office buildings.

THE FAMILY TREE

Christmas tree choices reflect matters of philosophy and taste. When your family put up the tree—right after Thanksgiving, on Christmas Eve, or sometime in between—depended in part on whether the tree was live, cut, or artificial.

Shopping for cut natural trees could be cold business, prowling the rows and rows of trees at retail lots, looking for one that had a straight trunk and symmetrical branches. But it wasn't as cold as going out in the country and cutting your own.

KEEPER OF THE KEYS, FOR YOUR TREE: A Cleveland classic—Mr. Jingeling ornament, circa 1970.

MAKING THE CUT

The Ohio Christmas Tree Association offers lots of tips for people who want to cut their own natural tree at an area tree farm. Some of the pointers deal with logistics, like measuring the ceiling height—and the width—of the room where the tree is to be displayed. Other tips deal with technique. For instance, tree cutter-downers and tree loader-uppers should wear gloves for their tasks. Cutting down a tree is recommended as a two-person job, whereby one does the cutting and sawing while the assistant holds up the lower branches to facilitate cutting.

Clevelanders are quick to share their own tree-buying experiences. Some of them learned the hard way about shopping for a Christmas tree.

THE CUTTING EDGE

God bless *The Plain Dealer*. They gave a list of places where you could go, places that shook the trees, bound them, and tied them on the car for you after you cut them. The first couple of years, our boys were kind of charged up about that. One year, as I recall, we picked and cut the tree in ten minutes. The windchill was twenty below that day.
—*Virginia Meil*

TAKE A BOUGH

We always had a cut tree because living in Cleveland, there was no real place to plant one. It was always a cut tree; you wanted to smell that fragrance, especially when the lights were on the tree. The heat would bring out the aroma.

When we moved to Brecksville in 1957, my dad embarked on getting a ball tree that we could plant somewhere in the yard. Many of the trees are still in the yard. There was one year when it was a tiny tree one of his customers got for him, and all the needles fell off two days after we put it up. My mother was just flabbergasted. After Christmas, my father dug a hole in the backyard and planted it. Today, that tree is about thirty feet tall. It recovered nicely.
—*Dennis Gaughan*

"I always disagreed with cutting trees down, so I've always bought ball trees."

SIXTIES STYLE: With or without the revolving light wheel, aluminum Christmas trees were a modern take on a classic.

LIVING PROOF

I always disagreed with cutting trees down, so I've always bought ball trees. The very first year I did it, I paid the difference for people who worked here at Tommy's Restaurant to buy a ball tree. I said, "If you're going to pay $30 for that cut tree, I can get a ball tree for $59. I'm going to give you the extra $29 if I can have the trees when you're done, so I can plant them."

Those trees are now bigger than the ceiling in Tommy's. I can take you to my yard and show you every tree and tell you what year it's from. Where we live now, there are thirty-eight trees. I put them all around. They're so big. It isn't that hard to do. I planted the trees, and they're monstrous now.
—*Tommy Fello, Tommy's Restaurant*

SPACE AGE SPECTACULAR

In the sixties we had an aluminum tree in the bay window in our living room. We covered its base with cotton batting that was dotted with glittery colored confetti. We usually decorated the tree with ornaments of the same color. One year it would be all shiny, solid-blue balls and another year they were all gold. The best part was the changing colored lights shining up into the tree. The colors were made by a revolving wheel in front of a spotlight. The wheel was divided into different colors of plastic film or something. When the wheel turned, it illuminated the tree in green, then red, yellow, and blue. The effect was very dramatic in a dark room. From outside it looked a little weird. —*Carol Lally*

SPARKLING NEW

I remember when I was ten years old, we moved from our older home in the West 52nd Street neighborhood to the West Park area. In the newer home, a ranch home, we had an aluminum tree. That was when we made the transition. I liked the color light wheel with the aluminum tree, and we had pink and blue bulbs on the silver tree. —*Josephine Kovach*

Family Christmas trees are more than decorations, though. They are also linked to memories of our loved ones and recollections of a particular era.

SPACE-AGE SPRUCES, A.K.A. ALUMINUM TREES

The color of aluminum trees ranged from silver to gold, green, blue, red, or pink. Their needle retention was perfect. They never needed to be watered, either. But that's not the main attraction for this type of tree. What brought aluminum trees into prominence was their streamlined, shimmery look that really brightened up a room.

FAR-OUT CHRISTMAS TREE: An aluminum tree in the Halle's window display, First Christmas on the Moon, 1967.

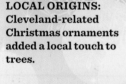

LOCAL ORIGINS:
Cleveland-related
Christmas ornaments
added a local touch to
trees.

MEMORY TREE

The best photograph I have of my mother is one of her sitting in front of our Christmas tree with a multicolor stuffed dog. It was taken in 1959, when she was 30. Her hair is in a beehive. She's alone, smiling and happy.
—*Steve Horniak*

PRESENTS UNDER THE TREE

I grew up in a very Jewish neighborhood and a very Jewish family, except for my father's brother, the infamous Jackie Presser, and his third wife. I just knew her as my Aunt Pat. They lived about a two-minute drive from our house in University Heights. They had a Christmas tree and Christmas presents under the tree. We always had Christmas dinner at their house.
—*Steve Presser*

TREES AS TRIBUTES

Tommy Fello recalls one of the Christmas trees he planted: "It is on the corner of Wilton and Somerton, where we used to live in Cleveland Heights. I bought it in 1982, the year my mother was diagnosed with melanoma. I drive by the house now and I look at the tree and remember that year."

BITTERSWEET CHRISTMAS TREE MEMORY

The year my mother passed away, it was really hard decorating a tree without Mom there. That's the year we got an aluminum tree. Older members of the family hated it. But I was seven years old, and we got this stick with holes in it that I could put golden boughs in, and I could do it all by myself. It was fabulous. My father put the tree—already garish beyond words—on an antenna rotor. It was probably about five feet tall, gold, and right in the front window. It beats the leg lamp in *A Christmas Story* because it rotated. We had red, green, blue, and yellow lights shining up from below to the ceiling. So you had this tree rotating, with different colored lights and green bulbs. I put a couple of ornaments on that weren't green because green and gold were great, but it needed something else. I had little porcelain bells that were my mother's. I put them on the edge of one of the boughs so that every time it went past the windowsill, it would catch—the little bell on the rotating tree hitting the sill. It jingled every time it went around. I still have those bells, and still put them on the tree. I would lie on the couch when the tree was decorated, the lights were on, and the rest of the room was dark. When I looked at the ceiling, I saw the patterns of the boughs and different colored lights. It was magic, and I loved it. —*Virginia Meil*

BY THE TREE: Jim Doney and Harry Jones of WJW, hosts of the Second Annual Cleveland Christmas Parade in 1969.

TIMELESS TREE TRADITION: Rev. H. C. Schwan, who is credited with displaying the first lit Christmas tree in a public place, is buried in Lake View Cemetery. Each year, volunteers from Hope Lutheran Church in Cleveland Heights decorate a tree at his gravesite with edible ornaments to commemorate the event.

A CLEVELAND CHRISTMAS TREE IN HISTORY

Back in 1851, Cleveland was the site of what is said to be the country's first publicly lighted and displayed Christmas tree in a church. On Christmas Eve that year, Heinrich Christian Schwan, pastor of Zion Evangelical Lutheran Church (then located at East 9th Street and St. Clair Avenue) held a tree-lighting ceremony at the church. The candle-lit tree was decorated with edible treats and brightly colored ribbons, topped with a silver star the pastor and his wife had brought with them from Germany.

Not all of the response to Rev. Schwan's idea was positive. Some were offended by it, and there was talk of the lit indoor tree being linked to paganism. Newspaper coverage of the day denounced the tree as "asinine" and "moronic." The pastor stood his ground and researched the roots of the tradition in his na-

MERRY MICKEY MOUSE: 1930s Mickey Mouse lights offered the Disney touch.

TWO SIDES TO EVERY STORY: Bill Hixson's two-sided Mr. and Mrs. Claus ornament is one of his personal favorites. "Behind every good man there's a good woman, and vice versa."

THIRSTY TREE: In 1968, Higbee's fifty-foot tree in the Terminal Tower foyer slurped up fifty gallons of water daily.

tive Germany, where traditional tree lightings were part of the Christmas celebration. By the following year, public opinion had changed, and the lit tree tradition in his church was established. Rev. Schwan served as the church's pastor for thirty years.

In 1975, the Rotary Club of Cleveland donated a Cleveland Landmarks Historic Marker that reads:

> The First Christmas Tree in America publicly lighted and displayed in a church Christmas service stood where the Cleveland Public Auditorium now stands, a designated Cleveland Landmark. On that site once stood the original Zion Lutheran Church where on Christmas Eve 1851, its pastor, Henry Schwan (1819–1905) introduced that first historic Christmas tree, a tradition he brought from Germany and which spread from that site throughout America. The present location of Zion Lutheran Church is 2062 East 30th Street—The Cleveland Landmarks Commission

Heinrich Christian Schwan died in 1905 and is buried in Lake View Cemetery. Through the 1950s, Clevelanders gathered there to decorate the tree planted by his grave. Today, Rev. Schwan's lasting contribution to Christmas in Cleveland is further recognized by the congregation of Hope Lutheran Church in Cleveland Heights. Each year on December 5, they commemorate H.C. Schwan's enthusiasm for Christmas trees by decorating a live tree at his gravesite. The decorations are edible treats: pinecones coated in peanut butter and dipped in birdseed, and strings of popcorn, cranberries, and macaroni for the wildlife at this 285-acre historic outdoor museum and arboretum.

DECORATION DAY

Once the tree was picked out, it was time for the fun of decorating it. The ornaments and adornments varied with each family, but the basics included lights, tinsel, angel hair, candy canes, and special ornaments with personal meaning.

TIMELESS TREE TRIMMING

I grew up on the west side, on West 54th Street, in the St. Stephen's Parish. Our Christmases were traditional. I remember trimming the tree. I would do the tinsel, a strand at a time. There's something about trimming a tree; to this day, I take the time to do it. First of all, there's the smell of the fir tree. You can't beat it. I could sit and watch a Christmas tree literally for hours and never see the same thing. For me, that was Christmas. If there wasn't a tree, it wasn't Christmas. —*Ron Newell*

LIGHT TOUCH

I remember how we would gather in the living room in mid-December to test our motley collection of Christmas tree lights, and how frequently we would endure considerable electric shocks as the aged wires shorted out in our hands. —*John Stark Bellamy II, author of the eight-book series of Cleveland murders and disasters, ranging from* They Died Crawling *to* The Last Days of Cleveland

LIGHT AND SHINY

Clevelanders bought American-made Shiny Brite Glass Christmas Ornaments, sold from 1939 to 1962, at Woolworth's and elsewhere around town. Max Eckardt & Sons started Shiny Brite in 1937, and the glass ornaments they sold remained popular throughout the 1940s and 1950s. Before World War II, the majority of blown-glass Christmas ornaments had been imported from Germany, Eastern Europe, and Japan. Made-in-the-U.S.A. Shiny Brite ornaments became the country's most popular glass Christmas tree ornaments.

BRIGHT AND SHINY: Made in the U.S.A., Shiny Brite glass ornaments enjoyed popularity in the 1950s and 1960s.

SHINY BRITE GLASS CHRISTMAS TREE ORNAMENTS

BUBBLE LIGHTS, 101

Many children of the fifties were mesmerized by the bubble lights on the family's Christmas tree. Like the revolving light wheel for aluminum trees, bubble lights were something you could watch for hours. Packages of Imperial Christmas Bubbling Lights, circa 1960s, came with instructions from the American Christmas Lighting Associates (ACLA). Here are some of the pointers: Always use bubble lights in an upright position. Bulbs must warm up for several minutes before bubbling action will start. Lights that do not bubble after the warm-up period can usually be started with a light finger-tap. A final note advised that bubble lights function better when they are not covered by tinsel or branches.

BUBBLE BUBBLE BUBBLE: A triple-pack of vintage bubble lights to dress up the family Christmas tree.

BUBBLING OVER

I had a fascination with bubble lights and also the ornaments that twisted in reaction to the heat. You mounted or strung them above lights on the tree. But there was this nervousness about bubble lights because of the legends about them exploding. You'd always be thinking, 'Oh, those lights are going to explode at some point.' —*Dennis Gaughan*

MADE IN THE U.S.A.

All the blown-glass ornaments were made in Germany . . . So Shiny Brite came into play. If you look at the Shiny Brite box ads, it's Uncle Sam shaking Santa Claus's hand. —*Joe Valenti*

NOSTALGIA DECORATIONS

I wanted to recreate the memories that I had growing up: the aluminum tree, the pink and blue ornaments, and the tree moving around. Vintage Christmas ornaments and trees remind me of the past. At Christmastime, more than any other time, you miss the people in your family who aren't here anymore, so having these things is a fun reminder of Christmases past. I think that is what draws me to vintage, what draws me to Shiny Brite ornaments. They remind me of my family and the love at Christmastime. You usually put Shiny Brite ornaments on aluminum trees, and pixies. They looked like little elves. I have an old felt tree skirt with Santa and his reindeer on it. It's made with beads and sequins and has pompoms around the bottom. —*Josephine Kovach*

THE MEANINGS OF ORNAMENTS

For me, Hixson's was the place that would put me in the Christmas spirit. From the scent of potpourri and candles, the amazing selection of ornaments and gifts, even the creak of the floorboards that would follow you throughout the store. I love the lady with tightly wound bun secured by chopsticks, a look I never attempted to duplicate, but always adored. My first Christmas tree in my first 'big girl' apartment was hung with many ornaments from Hixson's but by far, my favorites were the little elves made of slim pieces of wood, felt, and fluff. I still think of Hixson's every time they come out of the box and recall those leaner years starting out on my own.

TREE TALK: Bill Hixson talks with First Lady Laura Bush about a two-sided ornament with Santa on one side and Mrs. Claus on the other.

S ROZHDESTVOM KRISTOVYM: Merry Christmas in Russian.

BEHIND THE SCENES

Bill Hixson has designed hand-painted blown-glass ornaments for Christmas trees at the White House, and for nearly three decades, he has taken part in decorating trees there through five presidencies. "There are twenty-six trees there. The Blue Room tree takes between seven thousand and eleven thousand ornaments," he says. Among the ornaments he has used on the trees each year: a pig, which is a symbol of prosperity; a pickle, as a symbol of good luck; and a frog, representing progress or forward movement.

PIG, PICKLE, AND FROG: Ornaments that serve as symbols of prosperity, luck, and progress.

One of my favorite gifts to give newlyweds was a box of ornaments from Hixson's. I would carefully select specific types from the bins and write the 'legend' or meaning behind them. Glass bells with the frosted caps symbolized the joy and merriment of the season; coffee pots commemorated cheer to a new home; rabbits represented the renewal of faith during the season; the Christmas carp reflected the traditional German Christmas feast; birds and birds' nests were messages of love and good luck; and no gift was complete without the Christmas pickle, with instructions that this was the last ornament to be hung on the tree. The first to find it in the morning would get an extra little gift, or could be the lucky one to present or open the first gift. —*Marilou Suszko*

SMALL PLEASURES

My father would go out on long forays to get the perfect tree. My parents always bought a much taller tree than they needed, and cut the top off. My dad would trim the bottom of that, and put it in a tub—it was a little tree that my older sister and I had in our bedroom, and we decorated it with small ornaments. —*Pat Fernberg*

"My father would go out
on long forays to get
the perfect tree."

SEEING THE CITY:
Hand-painted skyline of
Cleveland ornament
designed by Bill Hixson.

ORNAMENT THEMES

As the owner and designer of Hixson's, Bill Hixson has collected the legends and lore of Christmas ornaments for decades. He says they fall into approximately a dozen categories. Here are a few of them:

• The Nativity—the Holy Family, the stable, the animals, the star, and the shepherds

• St. Nicholas or Santa Claus and his hat, boots, mittens, bag, the North Pole, the candy cane or shepherd's crook. Also, Mrs. Claus

• Snow, snow flakes, snowmen

• Old English Christmas, including food and the yule log

• German traditions, including the Christmas tree

• Musical instruments

THE FINE ART OF ORNAMENTS

Bill Hixson of Hixson's, Inc. in Lakewood first opened his business in 1949 and has been decorating trees professionally for more than fifty years. His experience includes not only teaching floral design classes locally and around the country, but also assisting in decorating the White House trees.

Today Hixson's includes a floral design school and a year-round Christmas shop. He shares some simple tips and techniques for decorating Christmas trees. "The very first thing you do when you decorate a tree is the lights. Second, do the garlands. Third, put in your accents on the peaks and drops of the garland. A garland comes to a peak, and right above the peak you have a bow or something, and below the drop you'll have a pine cone."

His tinsel tip works for family-sized trees as well as giant ones such as the White House Christmas trees he has worked on. "Down at the bottom you put the tinsel on one by one, then you group, group, group. When you get to the top, even if you're on a cherry picker, the tree is so large that you can't get close enough, so you throw a handful up and hope that some of it lands on different parts of the tree."

ANGEL HAIR-RAISING

One of the most popular decorative items coming out of the fifties was angel hair. It was packed in a cardboard box with a clear front, and was nothing more than spun fiberglass. It looked like cotton candy. It came in pink and white, and maybe in light blue. You were instructed to put on latex rubber gloves, not to touch it with your bare hands. You'd drape it over your tree when you were done decorating. It was non-flammable against the Christmas lights, and it gave the tree a satin look. If you remember the lights from those days, you know they were pretty hot bare-end bulbs, not like the LEDs of today. Angel hair was the last touch before the star went on. . . . And when you took down the tree, you couldn't save the angel hair. It went out with the tree and a bunch of used tinsel. —*Christopher G. Axelrod*

STOCKINGS HUNG BY THE CHIMNEY WITH CARE: A Christmas Eve tradition across the city.

Christmas Cuisine: The Ghost of Christmas Repasts

Food memories connect us to our childhood and our family. They also link us to our culture and our city. Some favorite Christmas foods in Cleveland include lunch at the Silver Grille or downtown cafeterias when kids went to see Santa with their parents. Many Clevelanders recall cookies, fruitcakes and Christmas petits fours from Hough Bakeries. Eggnog, delivered by the milkman or purchased at Lawson's or grocery stores, was another seasonal flavor. Mostly, though, we recall family traditions at our own tables. These meals were once-a-year extravaganzas, weeks in the planning. Clevelanders started early, gathering recipes, getting a head start on the baking and shopping, and enlisting the help of kids in the kitchen. Many families had dinnerware and tablecloths that only were used at Christmas. Some even served their holiday fare on the Christmas Eve pattern dinnerware from the Salem China Company, designed by Clevelander Viktor Schreckengost, the industrial designer who was a Cleveland Institute of Art faculty member for seventy-eight years.

KIDS IN THE KITCHEN

> My favorite time was polishing the silverware and dishes on Christmas morning. As we got older we were promoted to sous chef and got to help in the kitchen. —*Helen Wirt*

FOOD ON THE PAGE

Building up to Christmas, newspaper food columns were filled with ideas for readers.

About 35 years into her career with *The Cleveland Press*, Home Economist Florence LaGanke produced the newspaper's Christmas recipe book, *Holiday Recipes: Another Public Service of the Cleveland Press*. The collection offered a good representation of Cleveland's ethnic communities with recipes for baked goods, including Christmas stollen (German), Julekake (Scandinavian), panettone (Italian) and kalacs (Hungarian).

In 1955, Ruth Merriam, food editor of the *Cleveland News* ran a series of Christmas season recipes, including baked goods that seem a little odd by today's standards. Some of the recipes sprang from the English tradition, such as English plum pudding, and were a little, well, beefy. Among them were mincemeat fruitcake, lattice mincemeat pie, suet pudding and

HOUGH STUFF: Clevelanders brought home canapes, petits fours, cookies, fruitcake, and more for their Christmas celebrations.

FOR CHRISTMAS COOKS: The *Cleveland Press* Recipe Book.

BAKING IT: Whether they
came out of mom's kitchen
or from a local bakery,
cookies were one of the basic
food groups at Christmas.

English plum pudding. Mincemeat, of course, is the spicy fruit preserve that incorporates nuts, spices, rum, brandy, beef suet and cooked lean beef. Suet, also called for in the pudding, is solid white fat from beef and other meats. It has traditionally been used to add richness to pastries and puddings. Contemporary plum pudding, by the way, doesn't usually include plums. Instead, it contains raisins, dried currants, almonds, spices, and suet. The best part is that it's served with flame hard sauce over the top. The sauce is a combination of butter, sugar, and liquor—usually whiskey, brandy, or rum.

CHRISTMAS TREATS

Christmas cookies are definitely one of the four basic food groups of Christmas. Some of the other contenders are up for discussion. Eggnog and fruitcake have their fans, but they also have opponents. Christmas candy—candy canes, nougaty almond torrone, colorful ribbon candy, bonbons, and fudge, to name a few—is often high on the lists that kids compile. Christmas breads are another tradition, including stollen, the traditional German yeast bread with dried fruit and an icing made with confectioners' sugar.

SWEET MEMORIES

I remember ribbon candy—I was never a big fan of hard candy, but this stuff was good. And chocolate from Tower Candy. It always came in a five-pound box as a Christmas gift to workers at Fruehauf Trailer Company. I loved Lawson's Eggnog, plus it was a rare time of the year when some soft drinks were in the house. —*Paul Negulescu*

SHOW US YOUR DOUGH: CHRISTMAS COOKIES

Cookies represent family traditions. Lebkuchen, amaretti, galletas de Navidad and gingerbread men. . . . Whether you grew up eating rolled cookies, drop cookies, bar cookies, or pressed cookies, these sweet bites in all their variations offer a peek into family Christmas traditions. Sometimes the cookies came from neighborhood bakeries, but most often they came right out of the family kitchen. Cookie-baking is more than a memory of a treat. It's a snapshot of our childhood.

"Eggnog and fruitcake have their fans, but they also have opponents."

BEHIND THE SCENES AT HOUGH BAKERIES: Desserts and appetizers were part of Cleveland's party scene at Christmas.

BAKING DAY

Cookie-making with a two-year-old in the kitchen is really a project, but we hated to have Gail miss the fun. . . . We started out cheerfully but before the project was half over I was ready to run screaming from the kitchen. Gail slipped and fell onto the floured cookie board, she spilled a glass of water on the table with the dough, and pressed the decorations into the cookies with such force they fell apart. I had a long roll of chocolate pinwheel cookies which had to be sliced after being chilled in the refrigerator. I put the 12-inch roll on the cookie board and began cutting at one end—our daughter began eating at the other end. When I discovered her work, she had already taken several big bites from the dough. —*Janice Fleming Ghetia, "Life With Baby,"* Cleveland News, *Friday, December 21, 1951*

SERIOUS SNACKS: Leaving cookies and milk for Santa on Christmas Eve is a long-standing tradition.

CHRISTMAS FARE: Whatever you needed for your Christmas celebration—cookies, cakes, bread, mints and more—you could pick it up at Hough Bakeries.

LASTING TRADITION

Our family of eight children enjoyed the anticipation of Christmas. Our mother would fuel this excitement by baking, building, and decorating a large gingerbread house, always the week of Thanksgiving. The candy-decorated house sat in the middle of the dining room table, unsupervised and very vulnerable. Mom did this on purpose because she knew the candy would be gone in a few days and she would redecorate for the next attack. The gingerbread house lasted until after Christmas, then it was put outside for the animals to finish off.

This tradition rubbed off on me in a big way. Today I own Gingerbread Homes. I work with fresh ingredients to produce up to five hundred gingerbread houses a year. Over the Christmas season I donate houses to a few non-profit groups having parties, I enter the Botanical Garden gingerbread contest, and sell the rest. My main focus is to raise funds to support my sister's scholarship fund at Rocky River High School. My mother started a holiday tradition; I am sharing this tradition with a new generation. Thanks, Mom. —*Jon Thibo*

THE BEST BUTTER COOKIES

It was a family tradition. Every Christmas, one of us kids with a driver's license would cruise across town to pick up our "fake aunt" for the Christmas festivities. She was born in Germany, and always brought a shopping bag filled with several tins of her homemade cookies. As we arrived in Lakewood, she would always caution us, 'Put these in a cool place—they're made with real butter.' The cookies lasted well after the holidays, but the real gift was the details she'd supply on the long commute about her childhood in pre-World War II Germany. —*George Ghetia*

DINNER BELLS: Vintage Christmas tableware helped set the scene for holiday meals.

MEMORIES OF MEALS

Ethnic and family Christmas traditions seem to be most evident at the table. Sometimes, these traditions evolve, too. One family used to serve spaghetti at their Christmas Eve get-together, until the host moved to a condo with white carpeting. Then the menu changed to hors d'oeuvres.

Whatever is being served, the most important part is families gathering together for dinner on Christmas Eve or Christmas Day. In fact, these Christmas meals remain fond childhood memories even if kids don't always have a taste for the same thing their parents did. Some of the traditional foods fall into the category of acquired tastes.

OYSTER STEW

Our family had a lot of Christmas Eve traditions. We threw a huge open house for family, neighbors, coworkers, and friends. Because my mother didn't drive, my father was always assigned to spend all afternoon driving around. He had to make stops at Hough Bakery for canapés and petits fours, the liquor store, Lawson's for chip dip, Poppee's Popcorn in Lakewood for popcorn balls, and then he had to pick up things like ice for the shrimp. He was always exhausted on Christmas Eve. We didn't have dinner because we knew we'd be eating party food later. We just had oyster stew—a tradition in one of my grandfathers' families—before we went to the Christmas Eve church service. I didn't like oyster stew. I ate around the oysters, and just had oyster crackers soaked in the broth. —*Laurie Orr*

CHRISTMAS TREATS CHEAT SHEET

Fortunately, Christmas celebrations just call upon you to eat these things, not spell them. You don't even have to know what's in them to enjoy them, but if you are the curious type, here is a list of some of specialties of the season:

Amaretti: Italian light, bitter-almond-flavored macaroon-style cookies.

Buche de Noel: Traditional French Christmas cake named for the yule log it resembles.

Cornulete: These tender, flaky "little horns" are Romanian pastries filled with a nut mixture.

Flancate: Slovenian fried pastry.

Julekake: A Scandinavian Christmas bread

Kalacs: Sweet Hungarian yeast bread.

Kolache: These fruit-filled pastries are popular in many countries, including Czechoslovakia, have many different spellings, and numerous fillings.

Lebkuchen: A German cake-like cookie with spices and a confectioners' sugar glaze.

Panettone: Anise-flavored Italian Christmas bread filled with dried fruits and pine nuts.

(Continues on next page)

KOCSONYA

My mom's mom, Gram Soos, was of German descent, but she married into a big Hungarian family from Buckeye Road as well as its food traditions, many of which she kept after divorcing my grandfather. Hence, on Christmas morning when Gram arrived loaded with bags and baskets of gifts, she invariably had a covered tinfoil pie pan nestled somewhere within that housed the holiday kocsonya. We pronounced it kuch-en-ya.

Say kocsonya and you've just said jellied pigs' feet.

However challenging that concept may be, simply reading those words does not do the event justice. The shallow tin was filled with cooked pigs' feet congealed in aspic, which was essentially meat jelly that Gram had made from the liquid in which she'd boiled the feet. A generous sprinkling of paprika topped it off.

At some point during the course of the day, usually in the post gift-opening lull, Dad would get a cold beer, the Tabasco sauce and the tin of kocsonya. He'd pluck out a knuckle; which made a noise that I cannot sufficiently describe: just know it is the sound associated with a cooked pig's foot disengaging from a solid mass of meat jelly.

Kocsonya is a dish with very low curb-appeal.

My brother and I would watch on in horror as Dad dribbled a bit of hot sauce on the chunk, from which bedraggled bits of meat jelly hung, and then gnaw off the aspic and meat. Despite Dad's otherwise polite and careful eating habits, he could not execute the consumption of kocsonya without an unfortunate slurp or two. When the bone was picked clean, he'd set it aside on a plate or napkin and pluck out another piece. The whole operation was punctuated with slugs of beer.

The annual kocsonya affair was one of the fondest communications between Gram and Dad, sort of an unspoken understanding. Gram, Dad and my brother are gone now, but this Christmas memory endures.

Perhaps the time has come for me to make kocsonya, and horrify my own daughter with the spectacle. —*Erin O'Brien, author of* The Irish Hungarian Guide to the Domestic Arts

DAD AS CHEF

My father was always the person designated to make Christmas meals. He had all kinds of grinders for grinding meat. It was a process he started the afternoon before, and by the time we had Christmas dinner—breads, turkey, ham, sausages—he had made everything himself. It was always kind a marvel just to watch him. He loved cooking, and it was one of the high points of our day.

Of course, we always woke up at the crack of dawn to see what was under the tree. Even when we ate breakfast, there was always kind of a surprise. I can remember one Christmas when we had sausage and eggs for breakfast and for some reason the eggs were creamier than I could ever recall them being. I asked, 'What did you do to them?' My father said, 'Well, I put hog brain in them. Do you like them?' I said I did, but I wished I hadn't asked that question. So it was always a surprise. I remember the first time he bought a couple of tubs of chitterlings—essentially they're hog intestines. This was for Christmas dinner, and he was cooking them. We asked what they were and he said, 'They're chitlins.' Then he looked at us kids for a moment and said, 'Nah, you guys wouldn't want them.' And the God's honest truth is, he ate every last one of them himself. He just knew we weren't going to like that. He was probably right. But for the most part, Christmas dinners were turkey, ham, all kinds of sausages and dressings, and sometimes we'd have rabbit or duck. There were all kinds of rare foods that we normally didn't have—and we had a pretty diverse diet. All kinds of things would be set on the table for Christmas, and I always enjoyed it.

—*Reginald Carter*

PORK AND SAUERKRAUT

We went to midnight Mass at St. Mary's church in Collinwood. You were supposed to fast on Christmas Eve. After midnight Mass, the fasting was over, and we'd have pork and sauerkraut—pork chops, Slovenian smoked sausages, pork ribs. Growing up, I was not a big sauerkraut fan.

—*Joe Valencic*

Many Clevelanders of various ethnic backgrounds observe Christmas Eve with a meatless meal before midnight Mass, following the traditional fasting during Advent. Polish families, for example, often celebrate the *Wigilia* (meaning 'waiting' or 'vigil') meal with mushroom soup and other fare; some Italian families host a Feast of the Seven Fishes, with a fish-based, meatless menu.

FEAST OF THE SEVEN FISHES

Our family (DiLauro, Anguilano, and extended) continues to celebrate the 'Feast of the Seven Fishes' on Christmas Eve. The fish offerings are varied, depending on who is hosting the dinner, except for the squid salad, baccala [dried salt cod] salad, and fried smelt. In addition to the fish, we always make pizza frita (fried dough) and top them with a variety of things—sugar, melted chocolate, melted cheese—or stuff them with anchovies or peppers.

—*Michael Angelo DiLauro*

(Continued)

Petits Fours: Clevelanders remember the Hough Bakeries version of these bite-sized cakes, iced and eye-catchingly decorated for Christmas.

Pfeffernüesse: The name is German for "peppernuts." These marble-shaped cookies are flavored with cinnamon, cardamom, ginger, and black pepper.

Potica: Slovenian rolled yeast pastry with walnut filling.

Stollen: A rich German yeast bread filled with dried fruit and topped with confectioners' sugar icing.

Turron: Spanish nougat candy with almonds. Torrone is the Italian version.

MORE FEAST OF THE SEVEN FISHES

For the Feast of the Seven Fishes, you make it according to what people like. I grew up in the East 110th and Woodland area, and remember going to Gallucci's at the old Central Market to buy all our fish and vegetables, olives, and cheese to get ready for Christmas Eve.

On the morning of Christmas Eve, my mother would start cooking smelts, one of the fish. We bought them frozen, so my job was to clean them and my hands would be frozen when I was finished. I was probably eight or ten years old. We deep-fried smelts in a batter made with flour, water, and beer. My mother would make anchovies in oil, and cut blocks of haddock into pieces, make batter for it, and deep-fry it.

My father liked eel, and he was the only one who ate it. I always remember my mother saying it had a lot of bones in it. Maybe that's why they had seven fishes—because it's to taste. We also had codfish, baccala, that you had to soak for three days to get all the salt out of it. We never used shellfish, maybe because it was too expensive.

We also had vegetables, olives, and cheese. We ended dinner with cookies, nuts in the shell, apples, oranges, and then a ring of dried figs. A lot of times peope didn't eat them, but we bought them every year. The main part was sitting around the table. As people came in the door, there was always food on the table to help themselves to. To me, when I think about good times, it's always sitting around the dining room table.

I remember helping my mother prepare for Christmas Eve. She loved it, but it was a lot of work. She just made Christmas so happy; she decorated and cooked, and instilled in me my great love for Christmas. —*Marie Sandru*

CELEBRATING CHRISTMAS EVE'S TRADITIONAL POLISH *WIGILIA* MEAL

The celebration of the Polish *Wigilia* goes back centuries, and it's probably one of the most popular Polish traditions. In the church's view, the day before any holy day was always a meatless meal, and in this case, the holy day is Christmas.

We followed that rule growing up, eating a meatless meal that night, but even after the rule was lifted in the post-Vatican II Church, we continued eating traditional Polish *Wigilia* fare for our Christmas Eve dinner. I remember my mom and dad hosting the *Wigilia* celebration in our tiny house in the old neighborhood. Our dining room wasn't big enough for everybody, so to accommodate all of the guests we set up three or four long *Wigilia* tables in the basement for all of the visiting cousins and relatives.

Before the meal begins, the Christmas wafer, *oplatki*, is shared with each other. We break the *oplatki*, share it, wish each other a 'Merry Christmas,' say 'I love you,' and maybe even 'I'm sorry,' because it is also a time of reconciliation. We continue to celebrate this tradition each year and we remember in our prayers the deceased relatives, those relatives back in Europe, the poor, and the homeless.

Our family begins the meal with a thin-broth mushroom soup because that was customary for the region my grandparents came from. Some Poles prepare a beet soup for *Wigilia*, but our tradition has always been mushroom soup. Then comes the herring, either in vinegar or cream. Most of the kids in the family don't enjoy that. It's followed by cabbage and noodles, pierogies, beets, and fish—lots of carbohydrates! The fish we serve is always perch. My Uncle Joe is now the patriarch of the family, and as a fisherman, he supplies it. During the summer he fishes in Lake Erie and his catch is cleaned and frozen right away. Part of it is always reserved for *Wigilia*.

After dinner we sing Polish and English Christmas carols. My son and I sing them in Polish—for a young Polish-American, he actually is pretty good at them, remembering the words and pronouncing them so well. Other family members join in when they know various phrases or occasional words. We open up presents one by one, and when all of the festivities are done, there is the lull after cleaning up the dishes and getting ready for midnight Mass, where you're tempted to fall asleep for the night. But you rally and drive to church. Midnight Mass at Polish churches can go on for a long time because the scriptures and homily are offered in both Polish and English. After Mass and after all of the joyous well-wishing and reunions of parishioners is over and the church empties out (which takes quite awhile), we leave for home and that is close to 2 a.m.

The Christmas Eve *Wigilia* is a much more celebrated day than Christmas Day. Families get together on the 25th but the nostalgia and spirit of *Wigilia* makes the evening of December 24th much more special for Poles and Polish-Americans. —*Richard Konisiewicz*

THE 'BUBULKI' DINNER

A Slovak tradition which my family still practices is the traditional Christmas Eve supper, which we call the '*Bubulki*' dinner. In the tradition of abstinence from meat, each dish has a significance for the year to come. For instance, *bubulki* is actually poppy seed-covered dough balls in honey, in order to enjoy the 'sweetness' of life in years to come. —*Robert Tayek*

STAMPING IT

Trading stamps were yesteryear's version of shoppers' reward points. And several local grocery store chains got into the act. In the 1960s, Pick-N-Pay supermarkets gave out Eagle Stamps to customers who made purchases at the store. Shoppers could redeem the stamps for items at May Company. Kroger's gave TV (Top Value) stamps that customers redeemed for items in the Top Value catalog.

In the 1950s, for example, stamp-savers were able to redeem two books of TV Stamps for a Radio Super Coaster Wagon or a set of latex-body and vinyl-head twin dolls in matching outfits. A Howdy Doody toy marionette with a movable mouth could be had for a single book of stamps.

ONE FAMILY'S TRADITIONAL SLOVAK CHRISTMAS EVE CELEBRATION

We have about forty family members over for our meatless Christmas Eve Dinner. The table is set elaborately. We have a bowl of mixed nuts and a bowl of assorted fresh fruits, a bowl of stewed prunes and a bowl of mixed dried fruits. There are wine glasses, and on every soup plate there is oplatky, Christmas wafers imprinted with a Christmas scene. We buy them at Saints Cyril and Methodius Church, now Transfiguration Parish, in Lakewood.

The meal progression begins with the oplatky Christmas wafers and honey, lots of wine, an apple, fresh garlic, peeled and shaved into thin slices as it is served, mushroom soup, pagach (a raised yeast dough filled with sauerkraut or cheese filling), *bobalky* (dough balls that you soften and mix with other ingredients), sauerkraut, nuts, and fruit.

Everybody has their own way of doing it. We call everybody to dinner at three big tables. We start out with a prayer, toasting with wine, and then we pass around the oplatky smeared with honey. While that is going on, usually

MAINTAINING THE TURKEY TRADITION: In 1965, the AFL-CIO donated Christmas turkeys to 600 workers on strike at two area Harshaw Chemical Company plants.

the matriarch takes a dish of honey and blesses everybody with a cross on their forehead, to stay sweet during the year. We always get a sweet bread from Elmwood Bakery in Lakewood. Then we peel the garlic, sliver it, and pass bread on the plate with it and eat it that way.

Next, we slice the nicest apple into slices and the tradition is that nobody takes the last slice. Much wine is being drunk, and the oplatky, apple, garlic, and bread are gone already. Then we go onto the soup. My mushroom soup is served over coarsely mashed potatoes, about fifteen pounds of them. After the soup comes the pirohy—potato, prune, and mushroom. At some time during the meal—my husband used to do it and now my oldest son does it—my son Rick takes a handful of nuts and throws them around the room, says a Slovak Christmas poem that calls the mice out to eat, as it is Christmas Eve and they shouldn't be hungry.

After that, we have stewed prunes and then we go downstairs to the piano and sing Christmas carols, and have nut rolls and poppy seed rolls. We sing until it gets late, and the last song is "The Twelve Days of Christmas. —*Arlene M. Sterba (Arlene M. Sterba passed away on August 25, 2012, shortly after sharing her family Christmas memory.)*

There is no one tradition when it comes to Christmas fare. Cleveland tables were replete with roast beef, ham, turkey, pork, pasta, and more.

PHEASANT AND HASENPFEFFER

At Christmas we'd usually have either pheasant or rabbit because my father would go hunting during hunting season, and we'd freeze them. I think my dad had a twelve-gauge shotgun, double-barrel. The hasenpfeffer was marvelous. The only thing is, you had to pick out those BBs, and as good as you thought you were, there would always be one in the meal, so you had to watch for that. —*Virginia Meil*

"The hasenpfeffer was marvelous."

PORK FOR CHRISTMAS DINNER

For Romanians, it's traditional to have something with pork at Christmas—sausage or *sarmale* (stuffed cabbage) with pork. Growing up, all my Christmases were Depression Christmases. In 1930 it was a terrible year, in the depths of the Depression. I was about six years old. My mother said she'd never forget Father John Trutza [of St. Mary's Romanian Orthodox Church], because he saw to it that we had pork at Christmas. We had four farmers in our parish, and they did the butchering. Every big family in the parish had pork that Christmas. Not having pork at Christmas was unthinkable; for my mother and father, there would have been no Christmas.

One thing my mother made at holidays that was a treat were her own noodles for chicken noodle soup. She rolled the dough out very thin, maybe 1/32 or 1/16 of an inch. She had a clean white tablecloth and she'd put the rolled-out dough on the dining room table to let it dry, a circle of about twenty-four inches in diameter. Then she would start folding it, and folded it into flat pieces at two-inch intervals. She would cut the noodles, and did it very, very rapidly. It was so thin, and I used to watch her and wonder how she kept from cutting her fingers. The knife went up and down against her knuckles. She would put an entire chicken in a pot, cut up; there was a lot of chicken to make that soup. She did the chicken first, took it out, then did the vegetables—carrots, parsnips and celery. It was a very rich stock; she seasoned it and then put the noodles in. Soup was the first course at holiday time. —*Mary Ghetia*

NANA AND THE CHRISTMAS EVE ROAST BEEF

For several decades, my parents hosted a Christmas Eve dinner party. My father was entertainment editor of *The Plain Dealer*, and his guest list was a *Who's Who* of newspaper people, doctors, lawyers, artists, actors, and

ROAST BEEF RESCUER:
Dorothy Fuldheim Junior, who tried to save the Christmas roast.

CHRISTMAS EVE DINNER GUEST:
Dorothy Fuldheim

relatives. From the time I was eight until my early adulthood, our next door neighbor was Dorothy Fuldheim, the nationally known WEWS-TV Channel 5 news commentator. She and her daughter, Dorothy Fuldheim, Jr., affectionately known as DFJ, rounded out our Christmas Eve guest list.

My father often spoke of the division of labor, and on Christmas Eve day, that meant my mother did all the cooking, the children set the tables and cleaned, and my father wrote the soon-to-be-cherished Christmas notes. My mother's Christmas Eve dinner always included standing rib roast, a shrimp dish, scalloped potatoes, asparagus, French bread, salad, escalloped apples, a sideboard burdened with desserts, and Champagne. When the guest list grew to about thirty people, my mother decided she needed two roasts, one large and one small.

One harried Christmas Eve, my mother pulled the smaller cooked roast beef out of the oven, placed it on the kitchen table, and covered it with foil so that it could cool while she raced upstairs to change clothes before the dinner guests arrived.

She was still dressing when DFJ called from next door and said, 'I'm looking through your kitchen window and thought you might like to know that your St. Bernard is standing on the kitchen table, grappling with the roast.' My mother yelled for help and we all raced downstairs to see our dog, Nana, sitting at the end of a grease slick trailing from the kitchen table across the kitchen floor. The dog was enthusiastically ripping chunks of meat from the roast. My mother was not amused. Our tradition was to have sandwiches of leftover roast beef on Jewish rye on Christmas Day; that year, there were a lot fewer of them. —*Stephen P. Bellamy*

A BEERY MERRY CHRISTMAS: Clevelanders could celebrate with bubbly in the form of beer, brewed right here, as suggested by these 1960s advertising placards.

BRING US A FIGGY PUDDING AND A CUP OF GOOD BEER

Serving bubbly at Christmas didn't always mean pouring out the champagne. Lyrics of the seasonal song "We Wish You a Merry Christmas" call for a cup of good cheer. Sometimes the cup of good cheer of choice was beer.

Clevelanders could celebrate the season with locally produced beer such as Red Cap Ale and Black Label Beer made right here —and promoted here—by Carling Brewing Company. The brewery started in Cleveland in 1933. Originally known as The Brewing Corporation of America, in 1954 its name was changed to Carling Brewing Company. The promotional slogans included "Happy Holidays Ahead," featuring a white-haired fellow reminiscent of Santa Claus, dressed in an overcoat, hat, scarf and galoshes with buckles, wearing a holly sprig on his lapel. Other advertising featured Mabel, of Carling Black Label fame.

CHRISTMAS CAVATELLI

My mom is Italian, so our Christmas dinner was (and still is) cavatelli.
—*Kathie Brown*

PORK DUMPLINGS AND HASENPFEFFER

My mother was Irish-Bohemian. We always had pork dumplings and sauerkraut, and hasenpfeffer—rabbit stew—for Christmas. We used to call it 'Bunny Soup.' —*Dennis Gaughan*

SHOPPING FOR CHRISTMAS DINNER

Any time of the year is special and memorable at the West Side Market. When I was researching and writing the book with my co-author, Laura Taxel, it was an often-repeated event among many families; this was the place that they had to visit when the family gathered during the holidays. From the atmosphere of the building to the spirit and mood of the shopper and vendors, it has become a holiday tradition for thousands of families. My own personal West Side Market memory at Christmastime was ordering an awesome roast from Vince's Meats that set me back a yard and a half (that's $150). I treated that hunk of beef like it was the Hope Diamond, guarding it with all the tenacity of a watch dog as I moved through the crowds until I got it home. And although trained in the culinary arts, I scoured all my books and references to make sure it would be perfect. Was it ever! —*Marilou Suszko, coauthor of* Cleveland's West Side Market: 100 Years & Still Cooking

THE AROMA OF SWEET ROLLS

One year—I didn't live at home anymore, my sister was in college and my brother was in grad school—we all came home for Christmas. We had very little money, but we pooled it to get our dad a slide projector. He would always leave clues all over the house for us to find our big gifts, so my brother said he'd make this gift special and do a follow-the-clues thing for my dad. On Christmas morning, I got up early to make sweet rolls and coffee. I started smelling something burning. I remembered my mom kept the Tupperware in the oven, so I opened the oven and there was the slide projector. The ribbon was all brown, but the projector was in Styrofoam, which protected it. —*Lynette Macias*

ROLLING WITH IT

My mother baked nut roll, real Hungarian nutroll, which took hours to put together. There was one year when she caught a horrible case of flu and tied a bandana around her face, like a bandit, so she wouldn't sneeze on the nut roll. That year, when she was carrying it over to the stove on a greased pan, something startled her and the nut roll flew off the greased pan onto the floor. I thought she was going to burst into tears. She picked it up, dusted it off and said, 'No one saw that.' —*Pat Fernberg*

THAT'S HIS BAG: Wherever he went, Santa handed out gifts to kids.

KID STUFF

Visits to Santa Claus: They Laughed, They Cried, They Got Into Line

Santa held court on throne-like chairs or in sleighs in department stores and took part in public events and charitable parties around town. When Santa showed up for community events such as the Shaker Square tree lighting ceremony, he arrived in style. One year he came in on an iceberg with a live bear. Another time, he rode into town on a double-decker bus. Wherever he was, kids were there, too. Sometimes they found Santa Claus a little daunting.

STANDING IN THE SANTA LINE DOWNTOWN

You know the basic story, but it doesn't all come together when you're four, five, or six years old. You're being told you're going downtown to meet Santa Claus, and you know he's an important person, but you're not really sure why, or why you're going to see him. Then you're standing in line with all these other kids, and you finally get to the front of the line. You're taken away from your parents and the security, and you're out on this guy's lap—a guy you've never seen before—and he says, 'What do you want for Christmas, kid?' —*John Awarski*

SANTA SLIDES INTO SHAKER SQUARE

About 1961, Shaker Square had a big promotion just after Thanksgiving—the arrival of Santa Claus. And one of the big anchor stores at Shaker Square was FAO Schwarz toy store. I remember being there when I was a

THE BIG MAN: A 6½-foot-tall Santa.

SANTA GETS BENCHED

SLEIGH BELLS RING:
Santa sat in this sleigh to
greet children at many
downtown stores.

SANTA AT THE WHEEL: On the West Side, he drives a taxi as well as a sleigh.

little boy, holding onto my older brother's hand and awaiting the arrival of Santa Claus. 'He's really coming! He's going to be here tonight, and he's going to light up the square.' It was kind of a sleety night, and we didn't know where he was going to arrive, but he was going to be there somewhere.

He arrived on the slate roof right over Stouffer's on the Square. The searchlight looked, and lo and behold, Santa Claus was on that angled slate roof. On a sleety night. He pulled the light switch, and the Square lit up and it was wonderful for thousands of kids, Christmas in the making. FAO Schwarz was stocked and ready to go. And Santa slipped. He slid down the slate roof and grabbed ahold of the gutter. The gutter stopped his fall— three stories. He got his feet in the gutter.

Horror rang through all of us. 'Santa Claus is going to fall to his death, and there goes Christmas.' We were out of business—the tension, the screaming, the horrified kids. But no—who saved the day? The fire department. I remember them parting the kids, saying, 'Move back, move back.' And the police were there parting the kids, and the big hook and ladder fire truck pulled up in front of Stouffer's. They raised that ladder to the gutter and Santa Claus got safely on the ladder with the firemen and came to the ground. Christmas was saved. Because of that, a small riot ensued when everyone ran into FAO Schwarz

"And Santa slipped."

because the fire department was now their new hero. Everybody bought everything that was fire-related—fire trucks, fire anything. The fire department had saved Santa, so it was like something out of the movies. Hollywood could not have staged it any better. It was classic. The slate—where reindeer dare not tread. But what a fun thing, when you think back on how much Santa meant to the arrival of Christmas. —*Christopher G. Axelrod*

Taking on the Santa role was an honor shared by many Clevelanders. Halle's department store preferred to hire off-duty Cleveland policeman—including Frank Kane and Tom Moviel (later known for being the first in-store Mr. Jingeling)—to play Santa Claus. There were others, too—lots of others.

HE'S EVERYWHERE!

Our Christmas shopping routine was to go to Higbee's, May Company, then Taylor's, Halle's and Sterling-Lindner. I could never understand how Santa Claus could be in all these different places. My mother explained that he had brothers and uncles who helped out during the busy times. That solved the mystery of how there could be different Santas at different places during the same visit downtown. There was the traditional photograph taken on Santa's knee, but the big deal was the 25-cent present, the giveaway present that you got. —*Dennis Gaughan*

Not only did Santa hang out at Cleveland-area department stores and take part in parades, he was a party animal, too. He made the rounds of parish halls, fraternal lodges, community centers and local organizations. And all of this was before his busiest night of the year, Christmas Eve.

SANTA SIGHTINGS

In the late 1950s and throughout the 1960s, my dad, Bob Kosik, and many men of Sts. Cyril and Methodius parish made up the Catholic War Veterans Post 579. All had served either in World War II or the Korean War. Young men with young families, they would organize picnics and lots of events for our families to enjoy.
The Christmas party in the parish social hall was one of the best. Santa (a.k.a. Mr. Grospitch by virtue of his girth) would make an appearance and sit up on the stage calling out the names of the kids to come up and get a

HE'S HERE: Santa at the May Company.

YOU'RE NEVER TOO OLD: Santa at May Company demonstrates his universal appeal.

pre-Christmas gift. Of course, everyone got one but still you could hear a pin drop and feel the youthful anxiety building until your own name was called. It's funny, I don't recall any of the gifts I received but I do remember the anticipation. In the world of a six-year-old, it was gripping. The most memorable year was the one where a mother brought her son with a full-blown case of measles—everyone got an extra Christmas gift that year.
—*Marilou Suszko*

SANTA UNDER SCRUTINY

I'm a native Clevelander and I grew up in the Central neighborhood. Central is an old neighborhood, predominantly African American. Although many would have considered this to be kind of a poor community, we never saw ourselves as being poor. It was just a typical American neighborhood.

I remember one Christmas in particular where there was a neighborhood center on the corner of East 76th and Central. It was operated by the Salvation Army. We called it the Red Shield. They invited the neighborhood kids to come and meet Santa Claus and there were going to be free gifts and just a day of fun. My brothers and sisters and I attended. They had a recreation room down the basement, and I can remember there were probably 200 kids there that afternoon and we were all anxiously waiting for Santa Claus.

Someone announced that Santa had arrived, and Santa just bounded into the room with his sack of toys and started handing out toys to the kids, who were just going crazy. They were jumping up and down and we were all swept up in the moment. I stopped for a moment, and I looked at Santa Claus. It was the first time I had ever seen a black Santa Claus, someone who looked like me. I found it curious because all the Santa Clauses I had seen up to that point, either in books or on television, or when my parents took me downtown to have my picture taken with Santa, had always been white. And here we had a black Santa Claus and so the question as to whether he was the real Santa Claus came up. That was my first experience with a black Santa Claus, in about 1962 or 1963.

I checked out Santa Claus pretty closely. I gave him the once-over at least three times. I could tell his beard was not real. He had a white beard and it looked like it was made out of cotton. But it didn't really matter to us

"I could tell his beard was not real."

whether he was the real Santa Claus. We were just grateful and happy to see Santa. Everyone was so excited. Once the excitement kind of subsided, we noticed Santa Claus over in the corner. I think he was drinking some punch and he looked a whole lot like Coach Rodgers who ran the neighborhood basketball teams. So we figured out that perhaps Coach Rodgers was one of Santa's helpers. We had been told about the real Santa having lots of helpers, and we figured he had enlisted Coach Rodgers. —*Reginald Carter*

LODGE CHRISTMAS PARTY

I remember a great Christmas party at my father's Masonic Lodge, Gaston G. Allen Lodge in Lakewood. It may have been the year when he was Master of the Lodge. At the party, Santa had fabulous gifts for kids, with everything matched for certain-aged boys and girls. I actually got a Cox .049 Piper Cub flying model plane, in yellow. The box was marked "12-year-old boy." The girls were getting things like Chatty Cathy dolls. The year I got the flying model plane, other kids on our street got them for Christmas, too. We started a club called The Gas Guzzlers, because we thought the special model airplane gas was so expensive. Right after Christmas, we loaded our planes into a wagon and pulled them down the street to a parking lot near the corner of Rockway and Detroit, where we flew them. —*George Ghetia*

UNCLE JOHNNY, GRANDPA, AND SANTA

While growing up in Bedford during the '60s, we always had our Christmas Eve dinner at my grandparents, just a few miles from where my family lived. I was always fascinated by my grandparents' silver artificial Christmas tree with the multicolored rotating light. I would watch its glow change from red to blue to yellow to green (although I'm not certain if this was the exact order).

After dinner each year, my Uncle Johnny always had to leave to go to the drugstore to 'pick something up.' What, I don't recall. And every year, while Uncle Johnny was gone, Santa would come a-jing-jing-jingling along the front sidewalk, and we would hear his jolly "Ho Ho Ho!" from inside the house. We welcomed Santa into my grandparents' house and the youngest of all the cousins, which was me for several years, had the honor of helping Santa pass out presents. Santa always asked about Uncle Johnny, and we always had to tell him he left to 'pick something up.' Once the presents were

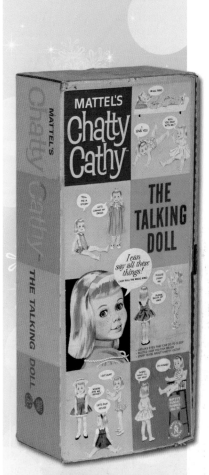

SPEAK TO ME: The talking Chatty Cathy doll, a 1959 classic by Mattel.

BEHIND THE SCENES

Ellen Dunlay's father, Frank Kane, was one of the Cleveland policemen who worked a part-time job as a Halle's Santa Claus. Joe Valencic worked as a Higbee's Santa while attending graduate school, and Christopher G. Axelrod has worked as Santa Claus at the Harbor Light Complex Christmas party, and at private parties.

SANTA DRAWS A CROWD: Frank Kane as Halle's Santa with Deb, Judy, Laura, and Susan.

distributed, Santa was on his way. Then, Uncle Johnny would return and we had to tell him that he missed Santa, again! Poor Uncle Johnny!

Decades later, while my wife and I and our two young daughters were living in Westlake, Santa began visiting us again on Christmas Eve. And this time my dad (a.k.a. Grandpa to our daughters) always had to 'pick something up' after dinner. 'Grandpa, you missed Santa!' our daughters would exclaim when Santa had left and my dad had returned. Poor Grandpa!
—*Joe Jancsurak, Twinsburg*

PRINTS ON PRINCETON

Before the age of unbelieving, post 1957, the Breslin kids knew there was a Santa Claus, not because he always left a plate of half-eaten cookies and an empty milk glass on the blonde maple armchair table. Not because their mantel-hung, previously limp red-and-green felt stockings were always filled with candy, fruit, and nuts on Christmas Day, nor was it because of the miraculous presents under the white pine. It was something much more compelling. Soot.

One December twenty-fifth morning, cinder-outlined boot prints led from the Breslin's fireplace over the clay tile hearth toward the tree. Somehow, the soot and cinders never found their way across the three feet of gold-shag carpet to where the pine stood in front of the picture window. That didn't matter. He was here! The evidence was clear and the kids knew it. The whole believing neighborhood knew it because they all saw it, jaws dropped, eyes wide, when they came to play in the Breslin living room that whole Christmas week.

But there was one kid who heard and didn't believe. She had yet to play at the Breslin house that winter of the year she moved to Princeton Boulevard. Beverly Weiner, who got presents for eight days in December, ate latkes, and spun dreidels had grown up knowing for sure that Santa Claus did not exist. When Bunny Breslin invited Beverly over to play in the days after Christmas, she showed Beverly the irrefutable truth. Santa had been there all right and Beverly's jaw dropped like those of everyone else. She ran home, wondering how her parents could be wrong. That night, Beverly decided to try putting a stocking on her fireplace. The next morning the sad stocking was still there . . . empty. 'But Mom! Santa Claus *was* at the Breslins!' Beverly's mom pointed to the Chanukah menorah and said, 'See this . . . this is us. The Christmas tree there [pointing to the Breslin house]— that's them!'

Although Beverly didn't try to put up a stocking ever again, neither could her mom exactly explain to her daughter what was on the Breslin hearth that Christmas. How could she know that Jim Breslin had waited for the

PARTY-TIME SANTA: Santa greets fans at the Severance Hall Children's Christmas Party.

SANTA AT STERLING-LINDNER-DAVIS

Christmas Eve fire to die down, took ashes from the fireplace, and dropped them around his big black galoshes, making footprints on the hearth? That he would delight in filming his kids' squinting faces as they came down the stairs the next morning, blasted by the floodlights on his Kodak Brownie 8-mm movie camera light bar. What Beverly's mom knew was that time would reveal everything. Indeed, as Santa myths crashed around them over the next few years, the kids on Princeton Boulevard came to learn that Beverly was right and that some dads were a little more creative than others. —*Bunny Breslin*

"He was here!"

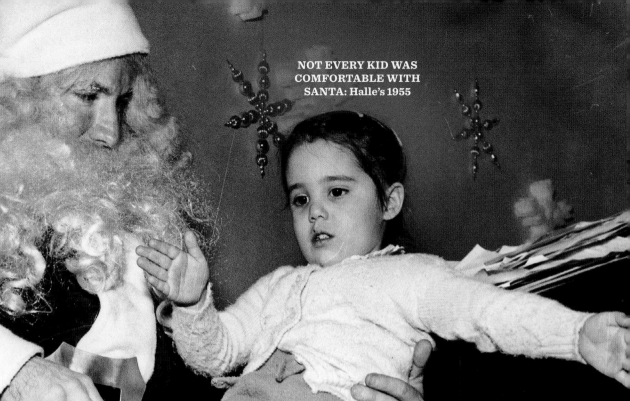

SANTA AND THE CATALOG

We didn't have a lot of money, so it was more than just ordering Christmas gifts. It was also an exercise in math and budgeting, though we didn't know it at the time. We were told that Santa had to get started making these toys and, because he was making toys for all the other children, Santa had a limited budget. It wasn't just a one-shot thing; you could go through the catalogs anytime before your Christmas letter was due, requesting gifts from Santa. Some of us would change our Christmas request several times. My parents reminded us that if we blew it all on a bike or roller skates there wouldn't be money left for anything else—so choose wisely. We looked through the Sears catalog and decided what we wanted. We were very cautious, but it was excellent because it taught you to think ahead and make wise choices. If you blew it all, you got one present. There would be other little things, of course, but that was your treat. —*Pat Fernberg*

LETTERS TO THE NORTH POLE

I can't ever remember wanting anything—there were some general things, like a bicycle or roller skates, and generally we got those. We'd write a letter to Santa Claus and my father would post the letter for us. That is how he gleaned what we wanted. We always had to write letters to the North Pole. We'd put them in the mailbox or my father would take them to the post office, and we pretty much got whatever we put on the list. We very seldom asked for a lot of stuff that we saw on television, but every now and then a toy like a Slinky would come on television, and we'd want one. Invariably, those would wind up under the tree. —*Reginald Carter*

HALLE'S SANTA

My father truly loved being a Halle's Santa. He was also in the Christmas parade. He used to go to the hospitals and homes for children. That was the biggest reward for him. He was built for the job of Santa Claus: God blessed him with the hair and the rosy cheeks. He was very down-to-earth, and a very kind spirit. He was jovial and didn't need any padding at all—and he had snow-white hair. My dad truly loved that job. And it was quite a thrill to see your dad in the Christmas parade. It was one of the joys of his life, being Santa Claus. —*Ellen Dunlay*

OHIO'S COLDEST

Christmas of 1983 was Ohio's coldest. Wind chill factors were close to -60° F on December 24, 1983, and Christmas Day saw these frigid high and low temperatures around the state: Cleveland, 1 above and 10 below zero; Columbus, 1 above and 12 below; Akron-Canton, zero and 14 below. The cities of Ashtabula and Conneaut in the extreme northeast of Ohio were snowbound, with Interstate 90 closed by eight-foot snow drifts. Wind chills on Christmas Day of 1983 were running near 50 below zero.
—*Dick Goddard, from his book* Dick Goddard's Weather Guide

SANTA AT HALLE'S

HAVE A BEAR-Y MERRY CHRISTMAS

Back in 1955, Santa Claus had some furry company when he arrived at the Shaker Square 22nd annual Christmas lighting and carol ceremony on December 2. Santa arrived on an iceberg float, along with Kelly, a 550-pound performing brown bear. The bear at Shaker Square arrived with his trainer. They traveled to Cleveland from Fairborn, Ohio, for festivities that included carols sung by the Cleveland Heights High School A Cappella Choir. The *Cleveland News* reported that the annual ceremony at Shaker Square had been attracting crowds of up to 10,000 in recent years.

Other bear-related Christmas tie-ins include Bizzy Bear, a comic strip by Ralph Eckhart and Edith Oliver Jones. The comic ran in *The Cleveland Press* in the late 1930s and early 1940s, and inspired a safety-minded Bizzy Bear Club in Cleveland. A Christmas postcard of the era wished kids a Merry Christmas from Bizzy Bear.

More bears with a local connection include The Care Bears, created in 1982 as a greeting card line by American Greetings, headquartered in Cleveland. The original ten bears include Bedtime Bear, Birthday Bear, Cheer Bear, Funshine Bear, Good Luck Bear, Grumpy Bear, Friend Bear, Love-a-Lot Bear, Tenderheart Bear, and Wish Bear.

Later, the Twigbee Bear starred in Higbee's local Christmas advertisements in the late 1980s, such as "Introducing Twigbee Bear: Cleveland's Very Own Christmas Hero." Twigbee Bear, according to the story, lived in the Twigbee Shop and became Santa's official Cleveland helper one snowy Christmas Eve when Santa lost his local street map.

HIGBEE'S SANTA

I was a Higbee's Santa Claus. When I was in graduate school I worked at Higbee's downtown during the Christmas rush. Among other skills, I learned how to wrap gifts perfectly. (The secret is double-stick tape.)

Next to the employee time clock I noticed a sign-up sheet for Santa Claus duty. I added my name to the bottom of the list, but didn't expect to be called. One day a supervisor tapped me on the shoulder. 'You're on in fifteen minutes.'

There was no coaching. An elderly gentleman was tying his shoes in the Santa dressing room. He pointed out a red suit and padding on a rack and a curly white wig and beard on a table by a wall mirror. There was rouge for my cheeks and a vial of white make-up to apply to my eyebrows. He handed me his regulation black Santa boots. Size nine. I wear size eleven.

I strapped on the belly and pulled on the suit, still warm from the previous occupant. On the third try, I jammed my feet into the boots and hobbled to the mirror. The wig and beard itched like attic insulation. I reddened my cheeks and sponged some chalky goo onto my brows. I swear it was correction fluid. I sported crusty white eyebrows well into the New Year. —*Joe Valencic*

TWIGBEE BEAR

BEAR ESSENTIALS: Care Bears made their debut in 1982, created by American Greetings.

BIZZY BEAR-Y MERRY CHRISTMAS

Today I get asked a lot of times to play Santa Claus. I actually have a professional Santa Claus suit. I am the Santa Claus for the Harbor Light complex. I have a great time with them, because these are folks who have been incarcerated and are coming home and meeting their families and having a wonderful lunch and some Christmas gifts with the children. It's a great time. —*Christopher G. Axelrod*

His Santa Claus appearances have also included private parties.

I'm not the traditional Santa, but I look like the traditional Santa. Many times I am brought in as a comic Santa Claus. I have a fun adult Santa story. Santa Claus is much like a rock star, and he does need the proper throne. And with those beards and that ungodly glue, the spirit gum, to hold the beards on, you need a water bottle with a sports cap so it'll shoot between the beard and the moustache into your mouth to keep your mouth moist. I was doing an all-adult party at a very large mansion with a two-story-high Christmas tree. I said I would need a water bottle, and a very secure throne.

It's midnight at this party of adults—many of them young adults and very beautiful women—and I'm in the basement getting dressed as Santa. As they were cueing me to make my Santa entrance, I asked if the throne was all set. They said, 'We don't have a throne. How about a piano bench?' They put the piano bench in front of the Christmas tree for Santa. I came up the stairs ringing, jingling my bells, carrying the sack of gifts through the crowd. Then it came time to shoot pictures. At the end of it, three beautiful young girls said, 'We want a group picture taken with Santa Claus.' I said, 'Oh no! No, no, no . . .' as they all came over and jumped on my lap. The legs of the piano bench snapped. I grabbed the girls so they wouldn't fall and we all inverted backwards. We rode back, upside down, and hit the tree. The entire two-story tree fell over, and the girls were caught in it, kicking and screaming, legs in the air, dresses up, and Santa was crushed by the tree. (Santa was fine, he's used to sleigh-riding so he'll roll anywhere.) It would have won *America's Funniest Home Videos*. The owner of the home said, 'By far and away, that was the best-talked-about Christmas party we ever had.' —*Christopher G. Axelrod*

SNOW TELLING: Regardless of the forecast, Santa had a job to do and he did it.

KEEPER OF THE KEYS: Earl Keyes as Mr. Jingeling in 1966.

Mr. Jingeling: Keeper of the Keys

Just hearing the phrase "Keeper of the Keys" probably reminds you, as it does most Cleveland baby boomers, of Mr. Jingeling. His in-store appearances on Halle's seventh floor downtown and his television appearances on the *Captain Penny* show on WEWS TV-5 are as much a part of local lore as Hough Bakeries and those thin glasses of frosty malts sold in Higbee's basement.

In 1956, Frank Jacobi of Frank C. Jacobi Advertising in Chicago developed the idea of Mr. Jingeling, whose job it was to assist Santa Claus during the Christmas season at Halle's. The character would also preside over the "Treasure House of Toys" on the store's now-famous seventh floor.

Frank C. Jacobi's "The Story of Mr. Jingeling: The Keeper of the Keys" explains that Mr. Jingeling was responsible for the safekeeping of all the toys made throughout the year for Christmas, and he was also the major domo in Santa's household. In his previous job, Mr. Jingeling had been a locksmith who made keys and locks for castles and treasure chests. Mr. Jingeling's keys opened all of Santa's doors—keys to the doll nursery, the train room, the candy closets, and book cases—and all the wind-up toys in Santaland. Mr. Jingeling also kept the fish-shaped key that opened Davey Jones' locker at the bottom of the sea, as well as the key to Pandora's box.

Tom Moviel, a Cleveland policeman, was the first in-store Mr. Jingeling in 1956. (In that era, Halle's hired off-duty police to play Santa Claus.)

The following year, Max Ellis was hired to play Mr. Jingeling on television. He was joined by Pat Dopp of the WEWS TV-5 children's show as the Play Lady. When he was selected as Mr. Jingeling, Max Ellis had already been pleasing Cleveland crowds in another capacity. As a member of The Cleveland Play

"Mr. Jingeling's keys opened all Santa's doors."

EYE ON THE PAST: A well-worn, much-loved early Mr. Jingeling ornament.

House acting company, he had won the *Cleveland Press*-Cleveland Play House best actor award during the 1951–52 season for his role as Willy Loman in Arthur Miller's *Death of a Salesman*. In December 1952, Arthur Spaeth of *The Cleveland News* wrote of Ellis: "He reaches into the heart of the character . . ."

Five years later, Max Ellis reached into the heart of another character and brought him alive for Clevelanders, when Mr. Jingeling made his 1957 television debut.

When Max Ellis passed away unexpectedly at age fifty, in 1964, actor Karl Mackey took over the Mr. Jingeling television role for one year. At the time, Mackey was the managing director of the Lakewood Little Theater. Karl Mackey was succeeded by Earl Keyes, a Channel 5 employee who had played Wilbur Wiffenpoof on *Captain Penny's Fun House*.

Earl Keyes (1919–2000) was the longest-running Mr. Jingeling. He first appeared in the role in 1965. Taking on the Mr. Jingeling role was a time-consuming pursuit. For example, in addition to doing the television show in 1965, Mr. Jingeling's appearances included the Euclid Chamber of Commerce, The Cleveland Play House, the *Cleveland Press* Christmas Parade, the Berea Christmas Parade, the Parma Christmas Parade, four Santa breakfasts, and the *Cleveland Press* Christmas party.

John Awarski of Traditions Alive, which today owns the copyright and trademarks of Mr. Jingeling, describes his first exposure to Mr. Jingeling on television:

I grew up in Cleveland, and remember watching him on television. My first exposure to him was on the *Captain Penny* show. I was one of the watchers. My mother would sit us down in front of the television so that she could cook dinner. Mr. Jingeling had a direct line to Santa Claus. He had the inside scoop. That was a different time and a different place. Kids were easily entertained with very simple things, instead of all the multi-imaging we do now.

Decades later, Awarski met Mr. Jingeling and learned first hand about how he became the Keeper of the Keys.

"Mr. Jingeling had a direct line to Santa Claus."

A number of us adults were sitting around during the holiday season reminiscing about our childhoods. Someone started to sing the Mr. Jingeling theme, which we all knew. I knew that Earl Keyes was the man who portrayed Mr. Jingeling at that time, and basically, I said, 'I wonder if he's in the phone book?' I called him up, and the fun part was that he was more than willing to talk. He was still going out and portraying Mr. Jingeling at Tower City and Penitentiary Glen, but not on a regular basis. He was pretty elderly at the time. I told him that I wanted to know how Mr. Jingeling became the Keeper of the Keys. He told me I would have to come over to the house. He lived in Rocky River. We set up a time, and I went over there. He invited me into his living room. On the mantle was his original set of keys. It was like, 'Whoa, there are the keys!' He made me, a forty-something-year-old adult, sit on the floor in his living room next to his rocking chair before he would start telling me the story. —*John Awarski*

STAMP OF APPROVAL:
Mr. Jingeling

MEMORIES OF IN-STORE MEETINGS WITH MR. JINGELING

Mr. Jingeling memorabilia that survive today include the cardboard keys to the Treasure House given out when Mr. Jingeling was at Halle's. Ron Newell remembers these souvenirs from his days working at Halle's in display and as special events director.

They would give away keys in the store, to hang around your neck . . . In the Santa Claus department, Mr. Jingeling would just sort of hang around a little bit and talk to the kids. But he got so big so fast that he became a real major part of downtown Christmas. —*Ron Newell*

Ron Newell discusses how in addition to television appearances, Mr. Jingeling's role evolved into other events. "I wrote the stories and John Petrone wrote the music for the *Breakfast with Mr. Jingeling* show. We had a breakfast in the Halle's Tea Room. Kids would come down to the seventh floor lounge. They sat on the floor in front of the stage, and the moms and dads sat in chairs in the back. That was around 1964 to 1967."

Countless Cleveland kids have stories about their personal Mr. Jingeling encounters at Halle's. Some still have their cardboard keys to the Treasure House. Others recall watching Mr. Jingeling on television. Virginia Meil first saw the *Mr. Jingeling* show as a four-year-old and convinced her parents to take her to see him on Halle's seventh floor.

UP CLOSE AND PERSONAL WITH MR. JINGELING

I remember the line that stretched all the way around the perimeter of the room. My father wasn't happy about having to stand in the line. And we were nicely dressed, so our shoes weren't comfortable. My father brought his Kodak camera, the kind where you looked through the top and it had an attachment arm, so he could take a picture of me with Mr. Jingeling. It was a long line and I was tired, but I was finally there. I looked up and there was the most terrifying face I've ever seen in my life. It might have been fine for TV, but this guy . . . the makeup was horrifying. I had a death grip on my father's leg. I was not going near that man. My father said, 'But you've been talking about this for weeks. We've just stood in line. Aren't you going to sit in his lap?'

. . . I was screaming hysterically, 'Get me out of here.' The people there obviously didn't want a hysterical child there, so my father picked me up and walked me out.

I do have to say that it's a part of our family lore. Whenever the family gets together during the holiday season and we've had a few adult beverages, somehow Mr. Jingeling of the exceptionally scary face comes up. And he was big, too. I'm sure he was a very nice man. He *had* to be a very nice man to sit through seeing all those kids. —*Virginia Meil*

The following Mr. Jingeling memory springs from the late 1960s:

MR. JINGELING MAKES A HOUSE CALL

After lunch at the Silver Grille we would always head down to Halle's seventh floor to see my favorite Christmas icon—no, not Santa, but Mr. Jingeling. I preferred him to Santa since he was a little less intimidating. All I know was that he was the 'Keeper of the Keys.' To what, I don't exactly know, but forty-five years later, I still remember that jingle in my head: 'Mr. Jingeling, how you ting-a-ling, keeper of the keys.' One year, my siblings and I entered a Christmas contest at the Halle building. My brother won the contest, and one snowy December day my mom invited some of the neighbors over. To our surprise, in walked Mr. Jingeling carrying toys for my brother. One of them was a red truck. A Christmas to remember! —*Lynne McLaughlin*

HALLE'S TREASURE HOUSE OF TOYS:
Where Mr. Jingeling was keeper of the keys.

Everyone had a Santa Claus, but only Cleveland had a "keeper of the keys."

MR. JINGELING ON THE FAMOUS HALLE'S 7TH FLOOR

My last Mr. Jingeling visit was in 1968 with a bunch of school buddies. We were 13 at the time, and were asked to leave. Guess we were getting a little too goofy and rowdy. —*Paul Negulescu*

ON A FIRST-NAME BASIS WITH MR. JINGELING

Mr. Jingeling knew my name! When I was five we visited Halle's seventh floor and Mr. Jingeling was waiting at the entrance to Santa's domain. 'Do you remember me from last year?' I asked. 'I'm Joey.' 'Why of course I do,' he replied. 'You're Joey! Now move along, Santa's waiting for you. —*Joe Valencic*

UNIQUELY CLEVELAND

My Cleveland Christmas story doesn't have anything to do with my ethnic heritage or any particular ethnic Christmas traditions, even though I am half Greek and half Romanian.

My brother Aristotel and I grew up in Windsor, Ontario, Canada. Our parents had emigrated to Canada in the early fifties, in the aftermath of the Greek civil war and the Second World War. They were denied permanent residence in the United States because of strict immigration quotas, so Canada became home.

We celebrated Christmas Day like everyone else, but we also celebrated St. Nicholas Day and Orthodox Christmas and even Boxing Day. We celebrated Christmas with all sorts of Greek and Romanian foods and pastries, too. Some years, we'd decorate the tree Romanian style, with candies and treats that we would later eat off of the tree.

In 1966, we were granted a visa for permanent residence in the United States. We arrived in Cleveland in October. Christmas in Cleveland was a lot like Christmas in Windsor—food, family, friends, and church. We went caroling with the Romanian 'colindatori' and attended solemn services at the Greek Orthodox church.

Mr. Jingeling was unique. Everyone had a Santa Claus, but only Cleveland had a "Keeper of the Keys." To me, Mr. Jingeling was what separated Cleveland from any other place and any other traditions.

WINDOW ON THE PAST: Mr. Jingeling doll from a Halle's store window display.

In 1971, my brother Aristotel—Tely—was a junior at Baldwin Wallace College. He and his best friend Jerry had gotten jobs for the Christmas season at Halle's. They were Mr. Jingeling's elves.

Their job was to herd the hundreds of boys and girls on Halle's seventh floor who had come to see Mr. Jingeling and get their cardboard key.

Every day after class, Tely would drive from BW in Berea to Halle's in downtown Cleveland. He was on his way to Halle's late one afternoon when the weather turned nasty—Cleveland nasty—rain and snow that turned to ice. The streets were slick and treacherous. There was an eight-car accident and Tely was in the middle of it.

He was very lucky. He was bruised and shaken up, but nothing was broken. He did, however, have a terrible gash across his forehead—the kind of gash that would definitely leave a mark . . . It took more than one hundred stitches to close the wound.

Tely didn't get to finish his job with Mr. Jingeling, but he did get to celebrate Christmas with us, and we all felt like we had gotten something very special.

For the rest of his life, my brother had a very fine, but very noticeable two-inch scar on his forehead. But he had something else, too—a story. Every time someone would notice the scar and ask what had happened, he was more than happy to tell them about Mr. Jingeling and Halle's and elves and Christmas and the accident.

WRAP ARTISTRY:
Mr. Jingeling gift wrap tag.

**MR. JINGELING AT TOWER CITY: Earl Keyes as Mr. Jingeling
took the tradition to a new generation of kids.**

HOW COOL IS THAT? Pete the Penguin puppet sang on the Mr. Jingeling Show in the later years, along with Ollie Daze.

LIGHTS, CAMERA, ACTION!

Over the years, Mr. Jingeling appeared on six television stations (Channel 5, Channel 61, Channel 25, Channel 43, Channel 3, and Channel 19) but the first was WEWS TV-5. The December 1957 *Halle's Bulletin* for employees gave details about the Friday, November 29, filming of the inaugural half-hour show on Halle's seventh floor. The article, "Mr. Jingeling and Santa Open TV Show from Halle's," listed the Play Lady, star of the WEWS children's show, as a participant. Students from Lutheran Memorial School were on hand to sing the Mr. Jingeling theme song. Meanwhile, here's the production schedule for the historic, first Mr. Jingeling television show. The Mr. J. Day countdown took place at Halle's.

- Noon: The WEWS crew begins setting up

- Afternoon: Students from Lutheran Memorial School are on hand to rehearse the Mr. Jingeling song they'll be singing live

- 3 p.m.: On-camera dress rehearsal takes place

- 5:30–5:45 p.m.: Last-minute cues are worked out

- 5:55 p.m.: Air time is called by the technician

- 6 p.m.: The show begins, and runs until 6:30 p.m.

On television, Mr. Jingeling's five-minute segments captured the imaginations of children who tuned in to learn about Halle's Treasure House of Toys. In 1966, the show appeared in color for the first time. That year, an estimated fifty thousand children—plus their parents—visited Mr. Jingeling in Halle's toy department.

That story was quite an ice-breaker and always led to more stories about Cleveland and Cleveland Christmases from long ago. And to folks who had never heard of Mr. Jingeling, that story was a revelation, a little window that opened on Cleveland history. Tely even managed to pass that bit of Cleveland Christmas tradition on to his own sons because even they wanted to know how their father got that scar on his forehead. —*Tom Papadimoulis*

THE STAYING POWER OF MR. JINGELING

Mr. Jingeling on the *Captain Penny* show was must-watch TV for me. To a young person, the concept that Santa would have a chief of staff was extremely plausible. Elves were known to exist, and to help Santa. The annual trek downtown was big in our family. Lunch at the Silver Grille and Halle's were always on the list. Halle's had to be on the agenda—being able to see Mr. Jingeling at Christmas in person, getting into a long line, filled with anticipation—and getting the key, which was a treasured keepsake. I do not have my original keys, but I do have a number of different keys from when Mr. Jingeling was at Tower City Center.

In 2000 I tracked down Earl Keyes and interviewed him for a story on WKSU. He was just so gracious, and I could see the joy on his face. I wanted him to recount the original story of Mr. Jingeling, which he did. He was so nice that before I was getting ready to go he showed me his memorabilia, including the original set of keys. It was the real deal.

In concept and execution, everything about Mr. Jingeling seems really well done and makes total sense to kids—the costume, the look, and the

INTRODUCING MR. JINGELING ON TV: Max Ellis appeared on WEWS Channel 5.

backstory. There was just a specialness to it. It was one of those things, like catching lightning in a bottle. It wasn't planned to last in the minds of Clevelanders for decades. Everything was perfect, even the people who portrayed the character. —*Bob Burford*

DID YOU KNOW?

• Originally, Mr. Jingeling was going to be called Mr. Jingles, but because that name was too similar to one being used by a television station elsewhere in the country, Mr. Jingeling was chosen as the new name.

• The green and gold Mr. Jingeling costume was originally conceived as being red, pink, gold, and silver.

• The original 1956 Mr. Jingeling song with words and music by Marian Jacobi did not include the words "on Halle's seventh floor." Instead, the first two lines were, "Mister Jingeling, how you ting-a-ling, Keeper of the Keys/ Does old Santa know how you're on the go and how hard you try to please?"

• In 1960 the bald pate wigs worn by Mr. Jingeling were ordered from Alfred Barris and cost $100 each. Alfred S. Barris of New York City was the wig maker for many Broadway shows.

• The first set of Mr. Jingeling's keys in Halle's were actually jail keys carried by Cleveland policeman Tom Moviel, who played the in-store Mr. Jingeling.

MR. JINGELING LYRICS

I.

Mister Jingeling, how you ting-a-ling

Keeper of the Keys

Does old Santa know

How you're on the go

And how hard you try to please?

Keeping track of Santa's pack

And Treasure House of Toys

And wind-up things that
Santa brings

To all the little girls and boys?

Mister Jingeling, how you ting-a-ling

With your many keys,

Don't you dare be late

For we have a date

Underneath the Christmas trees.

II.

Mister Jingeling, how you ting-a-ling

In your costume green,

Each key on your chain tells a
story plain

About the Christmas scene.

What a laugh when the giraffe

Found a key upon the couch!

He gave it to a kangaroo

Whose baby slipped it in her pouch.

Mister Jingeling, how you ting-a-ling

And the tales you tell

As you unlock doors and stock
all the stores

Everyone knows all is well.

SANTA BEFORE MR. JINGELING: Max Ellis as Santa Claus on WXEL in 1952.

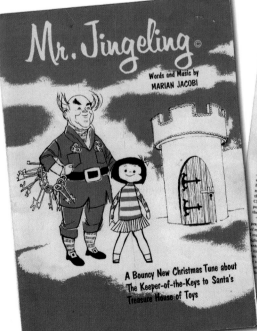

DON'T MENTION HALLE'S 7TH FLOOR: Lyrics to the 1956 original Mr. Jingeling song by Marian Jacobi did not include the phrase "on Halle's 7th Floor."

Toys: The Ghost of Christmas Presents

FAVORITE TOYS AND GIFTS FROM THE PAST

Each decade brought with it favorite toys, advertised on television, featured in department stores, listed in catalogs, and displayed in local toy shop windows. Favorites included dolls and bicycles, model airplanes and ovens that baked by the heat of a lightbulb. They were more than toys. Recollections of favorite toys connect us to our childhood and our era. Here are a few fond memories from people who grew up in Cleveland.

SOME ASSEMBLY REQUIRED

Some Christmas toys required additional assembly. That task fell to my older sister. One year I received a fully equipped Texaco gas station, complete with Havoline oil cans no bigger than a fingernail. My sister had to apply tiny printed labels onto dozens of cans well into the night. (For years after, the occasional stray can made quite a racket in Mom's Hoover.) The next year I got a Visible Man, a clear plastic model of a human with a skeleton and internal organs that fit like puzzle pieces. Once again, she was up all night, this time connecting bones and hand-painting each lifelike part with the enclosed kit. She got through the brain, lungs, liver and kidneys just fine, but it was the veining on the colon and pancreas that made her too queasy to continue. After that, I received gifts I could assemble myself, like a Kenner Girder-and-Panel Building Set. —Joe Valencic

BUILDING A FOLLOWING: Girder & Panel by Kenner, 1950s, an LP (Long Playing) Toy.

PLASTIC ORGAN WITH NUMBERED KEYS

One of my favorite Christmas gifts was the plastic organ with the numbered keys that my sister and I received as young girls growing up on Cleveland's west side. About four-and-a-half decades later, my mom still has the organ and we have the memories of passing the time waiting for the organ to warm up and then playing such catchy tunes as 'When the Saints Go Marching In'. —Debbie Jancsurak, Twinsburg

YEAH, YEAH, YEAH: Beatles dolls, circa 1960s.

DREAMING OF A WHITE ALBUM CHRISTMAS

The year the the Beatles' White Album came out was a stellar Christmas: I got a KLH Model 20 stereo to go with it. The Beatles' White Album was in stereophonic sound. I remember the KLH model number because I went to look at one in a local stereo shop after somebody recommended it. Before Christmas, I kept talking about 'the KLH Model 20, the KLH Model 20.' It turns out that my parents had actually already bought a Model 18, and they had to exchange it for a Model 20. My mom told me that after Christmas. It was a big deal, because it was a stereo. Previously we had a Magnavox hi-fi, mono, one channel. —*George Ghetia*

CHRISTMAS TIME

One thing I remember gift-wise at Christmas was my first wristwatch. It was like, 'Whoa! you're now a big boy. Your parents are actually realizing that you're growing up and you can have something of value, not just normal toy things.' This was a regular watch—no cowboy things on it. It was a real watch. —*John Awarski*

In 1959, the Jet Interceptor Fighter Cockpit by Ideal was advertised on television. It sold for about $15.95. This modern jet-age toy was promoted as simulating flight and combat conditions. It projected six moving "enemy aircraft" on the wall, and its rocket launcher fired rubber-tipped "rockets." The tracking radar scope flashed a warning light if you got off course, and it made a machine gun noise.

DOG & PONY SHOW: Steiff stuffed animals were great Christmas gifts, if your parents didn't make you put them 'someplace safe' and out of reach.

MOVES LIKE A ROBOT: Toy Robots captured the imagination of Cleveland's kids.

JET INTERCEPTOR FIGHTER COCKPIT

One of the coolest things I remember getting was the instrument panel of a jet fighter. On top of it, it had darts. It was a windshield with a stick, and as you moved it, a profile or section of the aircraft would move right and left. It had the sounds of the jet, a console panel, and a throttle you could move back and forward. I had always wanted to fly. It really impressed me. It actually had a little projector with a rotating disk that would project aircraft on the wall and you'd shoot darts at it. It was one of the coolest things I ever got. —*Steve Horniak*

Many of us remember the toys that got away—things we loved that somehow disappeared from the attic, succumbed to age, were given to charity as we got older, or became hand-me-downs for other kids in the family.

FAVORITES FROM THE PAST

My favorite Christmas toys were Patti Playpal, Chatty Cathy, Baby Pebbles, and the miraculous baby bottle with disappearing milk when you tilted it. I loved those. One of the gifts I wish I still had is a mechanical toy, Suzette the Eating Monkey. —*Laurie Orr*

Christmas really cooked for some Cleveland girls. In the 1950s, they used the pink Little Lady toy stove by Empire, an electric plug-in toy that had burners and an oven that heated up. In 1963 came the introduction of the Easy-Bake Oven by Kenner that baked by using a lightbulb. A 1968 classic was the Suzy Homemaker Oven made by Deluxe Topper. As advertised on television, this turquoise-colored stove had four working burners that each heated separately. In the oven—heated by a 100-watt light bulb (not included)—you could bake all sorts of things using mom's mixes.

HOT GIFT: Hot Wheels Criss Cross Crash by Mattel.

"I'LL DO THE THIN'IN' AROUND HERE": Quick Draw McGraw Private Eye Game by Milton Bradley, 1960.

SAY, KIDS, WHAT TIME IS IT?: Howdy Doody's Adventure Game, Milton Bradley, 1950s.

DINKY: The Dinky
Supertoys 972 Coles 20-ton
Lorry-Mounted Crane

SUZY HOMEMAKER OVEN

My best Christmas memory was when I was seven or eight years old. Santa brought me a new bike and a Suzy Homemaker oven. We usually got two toys from Santa, and they were never wrapped. That's how you knew they were from Santa. The gifts we got from our parents were new clothes. I was so excited to get a new bike. Most of my bikes were hand-me-downs. I remember making brownies with my new oven, and my dad telling me they were the best he ever ate. —*Noreen King Hone*

TURTLE POWER: Teenage
Mutant Ninja Turtles,
popular in the 1980s

HOT FROM THE OVEN

My sister got an oven—it wasn't an Easy-Bake Oven that had a light bulb inside, it was one that preceded it. It actually had a heating element inside the stove. It was really just like a little baking oven. One of my younger brothers who was still a toddler put his plastic pants inside and turned the thing on. Boy, that was the end of that thing. It was just a big fire. We put it out, but that was the end of that. —*Reginald Carter*

BARBIE HEAVEN

When I was of Barbie age, I asked for the Barbie Fashion House one year. It was my only Christmas goal. We lived on Halstead Avenue, upstairs from my grandparents in a small two-bedroom apartment. Our Christmas decorating included a cardboard fireplace with a real fake paper fire. We had just finished opening all of our gifts and I remember getting an avocado-colored bathrobe and an equally hideous strawberry print nightgown. I think I was pretty steamed about not getting my Christmas wish. My dad told me to go plug in the Christmas lights for the tree and there, behind the chair, in all of its cardboard glory, was the Barbie Fashion House. Lordy, I treasured that salon totally made of sturdy cardboard that now sells on eBay for about $800. Damn that damp basement! —*Marilou Suszko*

A 1980S KIND OF GAL:
Created by Cleveland-based
American Greetings,
Strawberry Shortcake
arrived on the scene in 1980.

HOLLER U.N.C.L.E: Napoleon Solo, The Man From
U.N.C.L.E. Game, Ideal, 1965, as seen on NBC TV.

GNIP GNOP: Gnip Gnop Game, Parker Brothers Slap-Happy Game 1971.

WILD CARD!: Concentration game by Milton Bradley,
as seen on NBC TV, ran from 1958-1979.

QUICK DRAW: The Etch A Sketch, introduced in 1960, is a classic with staying power.

PONY TIME: My Little Pony by Hasbro trotted onto the scene in 1983.

"THIS IS OUR MOST DESPERATE HOUR. HELP ME, OBI-WAN KENOBI":The *Star Wars* Princess Leia Organa, Kenner 1977.

CHATTY CATHY

My favorite Christmas present as child was a Chatty Cathy doll. My two best friends and I all asked for it one Christmas—and got them! My second-favorite would have to be a Pebbles doll, from the *Flintstones*, with a bone in her hair. I also remember Betsy Wetsy and Tiny Tears. Dolls were so much fun. —*Kathie Brown*

DISAPPOINTING DOLL

On TV in 1962 they were advertising this wonderful, wonderful toy you could get at the drugstore—a doll with curly blonde hair, with her own beauty parlor chair and beauty parlor hooded hairdryer and curling rods. I thought this was the most fabulous thing in the world, looking at the commercial. So I nagged and nagged. My father wouldn't buy it, but my aunt and uncle got me the set. They went to at least four stores to get it because it was sold out everywhere. It was the biggest piece of junk that ever came through the door: cheap, easily broken, ugly doll—and it didn't plug in. —*Virginia Meil*

SANTA AND THE BIG BRUISER

The ads ran on *Captain's Comedy Clubhouse* for weeks for the Marx Big Bruiser Tow Truck with battery-powered lights and towing winch. I envisioned myself coming to the aid of distressed motorists, hoisting up their damaged vehicles, changing flat tires, and towing them to safety. The jack and rotating flashing light above the cab were the icing on the proverbial

SPACE AGE: Star Wars Land Speeder, Kenner, 1979.

Christmas pudding. This, indeed, was the Christmas dream come true, for $19.95 plus tax. The Big Bruiser headed the Christmas lists I distributed to grandmothers, aunts, and my parents that year.

In the pre-freeway, pre-mall, far-flung suburb of Mentor, an object as grand and exotic as the Big Bruiser was not to be found. It could only be acquired on one day—the annual Christmas shopping trip our family made to downtown Cleveland shortly after Thanksgiving.

We visited Halle's, Higbee's, and the May Company. Time went by with agonizing slowness in the clothing departments. Then, as we investigated various toy departments, a nagging worry took shape. There were no Big Bruisers to be found. I overheard whispers that seemed to confirm this devastating fact. 'Pssst. Sold out.' . . . 'On back-order.' . . . 'Too late to drop ship.'

It couldn't be true. Santa wouldn't let me down, not when Big Bruiser meant so much. Surely the elves could make just one more. I calculated what I might find under the tree that year: new gloves, underpants and socks, corduroy trousers, and a shirt. Eight years old and the Grinch was truly upon me.

Each night before bed I asked Santa to come through for me. "Give to me the Gift of Gifts. Don't let me down, Santa! You know I've been good! Just one Big Bruiser for me. Oh, please."

On Christmas morning, there were presents under the tree and lots of them, but no box big enough to contain my Christmas dream toy. There were pants and socks, gloves, and shirts. When the opening was done, it was what I most feared: no Big Bruiser. In fact, no tow truck at all.

As I gulped back the lump in my throat, Mom went out to the kitchen and slowly walked back into the living room. In her arms was a small, white, whining poodle puppy, as cute a creature as I'd ever seen. I held out my arms to take him as she asked me his name. Blinking back the tears, I exclaimed, 'It's Bruiser!' —*William Small*

BATTERIES NOT INCLUDED: Bubble Blowing Battery-operated Monkey with Lighted Eyes was a 1950s toy by Rock Valley Toys.

HOT STUFF: Hot Wheels drove onto the scene in 1968.

"Don't let me down, Santa! You know I've been good!"

RALLY OF THE DOLLS

As any Cleveland baby boomer can tell you, each doll seemed to have its own claim to fame. The Tiny Tears doll with Rock-a-Bye Eyes appeared on the *Ding Dong School* television program with Miss Francis in 1956. The "life-sized" Patti Playpal doll was as big as a three-year-old. When you pulled the string on her back, you never knew what Chatty Cathy was going to say. She usually had a request, such as, "Please change my dress" or "Tell me a story." Tressy had "growing" hair and the Cabbage Patch Kids, introduced by Coleco in 1983, each came with a pretend birth certificate and adoption papers.

1950 Tiny Tears by American Character Doll Corporation

1954 Betsy Wetsy by Ideal

1959 Patti Playpal by Ideal

1959 Chatty Cathy by Mattel

1959 Barbie by Mattel

1961 Troll Dolls introduced in U.S., originally made by Thomas Dam of Dam Things in Denmark

1962 Tammy by Ideal

1963 Baby Pebbles by Ideal/ Hanna Barbera

1963 Tressy by American Doll Corporation

1969 Baby Tender Love by Mattel

HAIR-RAISING: Troll Dolls

UH-OH! IT'S BROKEN

There was a toy tow truck advertised on television during the Saturday cartoons, Big Bruiser by Marx: 'Hello, Big Bruiser? Just wrecked my truck.' It had a hook that came down and picked up broken-down cars. My cousin got it for Christmas. We were playing with it, and I think the hook broke off. Another Christmas, I broke the arm off his Rock 'Em Sock 'Em Robot by mistake, and I remember my aunt trying to put it back on. There was a woodshop toy of his that broke when we were playing with it, too. All we were trying to do was recreate the television commercial demos. We even knew the dialogue from them. —*George Ghetia*

ONE SHARP DOLLHOUSE

There was one year when I asked for a dollhouse, one of those sheet metal things that you have to fold and crimp, and force the tabs into the slots. Of course, the tabs never stayed in. On Christmas morning we woke up and I was thrilled to see the dollhouse under the tree. They must have wiped all the blood off the dollhouse at that point, but my father had a bunch of bandages on his fingers. Santa was good that year, but not that good to himself. —*Pat Fernberg*

MISS POPULARITY: Red-headed Cabbage Patch Doll by Coleco, 1985.

"Nobody wanted to play with you if you didn't have a Barbie."

Toys that inspired imagination included The Erector Set, the Etch A Sketch and the Lite-Brite lightbox introduced by Hasbro in 1967. In 1960, the Etch A Sketch went into production at Ohio Art Company. Reportedly, the demand was so great that workers at the factory in Bryan, Ohio, were still turning them out until noon on Christmas Eve.

MEMORABLE TOYS

I asked for a Barbie, but got a Tammie. That wasn't the same. Nobody wanted to play with you if you didn't have a Barbie. I remember Etch A Sketch and Silly Putty. My little brother was seven years younger, and he got a Lite-Brite light box. In fifth grade, I got a transistor radio. Mine was about four inches thick, about eight inches by eight inches. It was white with a white vinyl cover. I also remember Nancy Drew books, and *Cherry Ames, Student Nurse*, from the series of nurse books. I think that's why I became a nurse. My favorite gift was one I got from our next-door neighbor when I was in fourth grade: a fortune cookie–making set. —*Bunny Sullivan Trepal*

TOYS TO BUILD YOUR COOLNESS QUOTIENT

You were a nobody if you didn't get . . . an Erector Set, an electric train set, the Rock 'Em Sock 'Em Robots, or a Daisy Air Rifle. The gift of all gifts for a boy was a Schwinn Sting-Ray bike, especially if it was the Orange Krate version. —*Paul Negulescu*

THE BIKE

The most important gift as a youngster was a Schwinn Sting-Ray bicycle with a banana seat. I didn't think I was getting it because it wasn't under the Christmas tree. But then my dad brought it in. I rode it in the snow that day. The seat had that leopard print—those stylistic details stick with you. I thought I was the coolest and luckiest kid on earth. —*Bob Burford*

Toy trains are in a Christmas class all by themselves. This was one toy that parents seemed to enjoy as much as their children did.

NUTS ABOUT NUTTY MADS: Nutty Mads, 1963-64, six-inch injection molded plastic toys by Marx.

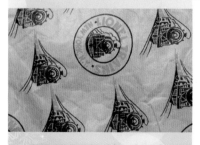

FOR THE TRAIN GANG:
Lionel Train catalogs like
this 1947 edition helped
create lots of Christmas
wish lists.

WRAP IT UP: Lionel Trains
came packed in their own
special wrapping paper.

ALL ABOARD

We had a Lionel Train Set and my father constructed a big table. I think he
was more into it than I was. We had twin tracks and twin trains and we'd
have train races. He took screen and plaster of paris and made papier-
maché tunnels, and there were little towns with people, farm communities
with barns and cows. I remember the locomotive: You put pellets into the
smokestack and blew the whistle. It would just chug along with smoke coming out of it and it was just like the real thing. It was great. —*Reginald Carter*

BUILDING STEAM

When I was young, my dad worked for Spang Bakery as a driver and he
saved his tips throughout the year. At Christmastime, he went to Vinnie's,
the hardware store on Lee Road, and bought another piece of equipment
for the train collection. . . . Early on, Santa always brought another part of
the train set. My dad was just as thrilled to see what was unpacked as I was.
He couldn't wait to put it on the track. I guess that's part of the Lionel or toy
train tradition: father and son playing with electric trains.

I think part of the fascination with Lionel was the wonderful catalogs that came out every year, with the seemingly endless varieties of locomotives. I always lusted after a diesel locomotive, even though I had several nice steam locomotives.

One of the features that Lionel had was the train that puffed real smoke. There was a little heating coil in the smokestack of the steam locomotives, and you dropped a pellet in there that would warm up and emit smoke—and not only just smoke, but with a puffing mechanism. As the train went around the track, it would literally puff and chug out smoke rings. The smell was terrible, a sweet, awful smell. You could only do it so long before the whole house smelled of the smoke pellet smell, but it was an intriguing system. —*Dennis Gaughan*

SHARED TRAIN

I remember my sister and I shared a Lionel train one year. It was 'The Whole Big Gift.' I got into trains. I'm still into model trains, and I still have that original train set. We had the train on the floor for a couple of weeks, and then we packed it away. —*John Awarski*

THE JOY OF TOYS

Nostalgia toy expert Steve Presser of Big Fun, in Cleveland Heights and on Cleveland's westside, discusses memories of toys from childhood:

The beauty of toys is that in a way they are a fantasy world for people. You can be the most timid individual or the loudest, but when you get a good toy you can play by yourself with it and have great creative scenes with things like doll houses to army men. Or you can play with others.

TRANSFORMATIVE:
Transformer action toys.

FIGHTING MAN FROM HEAD TO TOE: G.I. Joe was introduced in the 1960s.

ACTION AND ACTIVITY-ORIENTED TOYS

Five years after Barbie arrived on the scene, the twelve-inch action figure G.I. Joe showed up—a "fighting man, head to toe," according to television commercials. You could get uniforms and equipment to change the soldier into a camouflaged Marine ready for battle, a Navy frogman with complete scuba tube and inflatable life raft, or an Air Force pilot with a high altitude helmet and air vest. The Easy-Bake Oven came with its own Betty Crocker cake mixes that could be baked using the oven's 100-watt light bulb. In the 1980s, toys like Transformers and Teenage Mutant Ninja Turtles were on lots of Christmas lists.

1913 Erector Set by A.C. Gilbert Company

1960 Etch A Sketch by Ohio Art Company

1963 Easy-Bake Oven by Kenner

1963 Schwinn Sting-Ray Bikes

1964 Rock 'Em Sock 'Em Robots by Marx ("Knock his block off")

1964 G.I. Joe action figure by Hasbro

1968 Schwinn Sting-Ray Krates

1969 The Big Wheel tricycle by Marx remained a hot toy in the 1970s

1970 Nerf Balls from Parker Brothers were promoted as indoor balls (the name is an acronym for non-expanding recreational foam). Mood rings and pet rocks were big, too.

1977 Atari 2600, a.k.a. Atari VCS, video game console

1985 Transformers by Hasbro, whereby what looks like one thing transforms into another

THEREBY HANGS A TAIL: In 1955, "The Ballad of Davy Crockett" by Bill Hayes was one of the year's top songs. *Davy Crockett* was on television, and coonskin hats were a hot gift.

TOY DEPARTMENT PRICE CHECK

1951: The Toni Doll by Ideal Toy Co. was $11.98 at Sherwin Hardware on E. 185th St.

1954: Roy Rogers and Dale Evans outfits for kids cost $4.95 each at Halle's unless you wanted to throw in an extra $1.95 for a rodeo hat. The Roy Rogers Holster Set with two six-guns and a rustic saddle tan holster was $4.98 at Higbee's.

1954: Cinderella Timex Shock-Resistant Watches with leather bands cost $6.95 at Higbee's.

1958: Non-breakable Zippee nylon roller skates were $2.98 at Halle's.

1958: Dennis the Menace dolls were $3.98 (Kiddie Furniture Mart in Parma).

1964: An eight-transistor Fantavox Transistor Radio was $10 with a cowhide case at Higbee's.

The half-generation before me was the tin toy generation and I'm totally enamored with it as a collector. They're mechanical, a lot of battery-operated stuff, lot of attention to detail and packaging. I'm a big box art person. Sometimes the box art was even better than the actual toy that was inside.

Slowly we started to see the migration from metal to tin, back to metal a little bit, and then the grand departure to plastic. The plastic quality has changed over the generations. The plastics today, the polymers, are incredible. Right now, Legos are on fire. It's the same quality of plastic they've used for years, a good-quality plastic that holds up. Legos were one of my favorite toys. I also loved Lincoln Logs. I am not the most mechanical person, but give me Lincoln Logs and I can build you a city. The Erector Set spawned other generations of toys, motors, batteries, screws with nuts and bolts. That was almost a hobbyist-type toy, versus a play toy.

Davy Crockett was on television, and every kid wanted a coonskin hat in the late 1950s—and mouse ears from The Mickey Mouse Club. Shows in maybe 1964–1966 were the golden years of the first commercial blasts of toys.

Then the eighties literally had half-hour shows to promote products. There was a big hullaballo: 'Are these TV shows, or are they commercials?' Eighties kids got captured like no other generation before them. For boys, it was G.I. Joe, and *Star Wars*—that started in the late seventies but went through the eighties—Transformers and Hot Wheels. For girls—and American Greetings in Cleveland is responsible for this—it's Care Bears and Strawberry Shortcake. Holly Hobbie is a secondary one. Rainbow Brite is strong; Smurfs and Garbage Pail Kids are peripheral. —*Steve Presser, Big Fun*

ARE YOU GAME? The popular Atari model 2600 (1978) was on lots of Christmas lists.

GAME ON: Home video gaming systems became popular
holiday gifts as early as the the mid-1970s.

A KNOCKOUT GIFT:
Unboxing the Rock 'em
Sock ' em Robots!

TOY FUN

White House with Eight Presidents. Now for the first time, ...ntic replica of the historic executive mansion faithfully ...d to scale, complete with 8 exact miniatures of Famous ... 18 inches overall. **3.95**

...erne decorating set . . . walls to paper, furniture to paint, ...to make. Styled in House & Garden colors. Fabrics by ...her & Co. Just like mother's. Lots of learning-ful fun to ...reer. **4.95**

...Cash register . . . 9 keys to ring up sales, total lever, play ... metal, rounded edges, rubber feet, plastic windows. **2.95**

...ool table by C. G. Wood. Cloth surface, wood frame, 15 ...all, two 24" cues, triangle, automatic return. 25" by 17". **4.95**

69E-373—Doll-E-Shopper by Amsco. Tiny famous-brand packages in steel cart with lift-out tray an Doll-E-Seat. **4.95**

69F-373—Master Juvenile pogo stick . . . adjustable spring tension, rubber shoe, pads. Lightweight hardwood. 41". **6.95**

69G-373—In chrome steel tubing. **6.95**

69H-373—Friendly Folks Motel by Kiddie Brush. 75 pieces of travel fun . . . 2 suites, offices. Metal; plastic furniture, and figures. **6.95**

69J-373—Donald Duck Auto-Magic projector with batteries, 4 films. Projects on any flat surface. Plastic, by Stephens. Additional assorted films available. **2.95**

69K-373—Pressman plastic printing press . . . rubber type, ink, brush, paper, tweezers. Easy to print cards, stationery, "newspapers." 15" long. **3.95**

Toys, Euclid, Seventh Floor

Use the handy mail order coupon and postage-free envelope between pages 17 and 18, and pages 53 and 54.

69A 69B 69C

69D 69E 69F

69H 69J 69K

. . . their passports to the land

By SACKMAN

70A-373—Engineer. Hickory striped heavy denim overalls with matching engineer jacket. Railroad insignia on jacket. Engineer's cap, bandana. Even sizes, 2 to 14. **4.95**

70A 70B 70C 70D

70H 70J

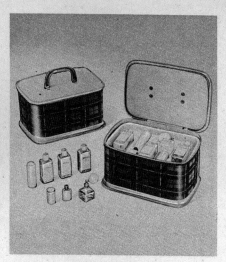

Captain Crow challenges you in this game of darts *by Knickerbocker*. He moves his beak, caws continuously and stares mischievously until your pistol-fired dart finds its mark. Battery operated. (81373A) $3.98.

Intriguing **Zorro Target Game** similar to above. (Not pictured). (81373B) $2.98.

She'll travel up and down the block with her Fitted Travel Case *by Amsco Products*. Red plaid fabric sides; tan grain top and bottom; zipper top closing; red handle. Grand lift-out tray with genuine, harmless cosmetics. (81373C) $5.98.

Make a real home run right in the rumpus room with this action packed Electronic Baseball Game *by Tudor Products*. Score home runs, hits, outs. AC current. (81373D) $6.98.

Thrill-packed **Electric Football Game.** Similar to above (Not shown.) (81373E) $6.98.

Toys—Seventh Floor and Suburban Stores

Halle's for Wonderful Toys

Aspiring young musicians adore Emenee instruments. Creates an interest in music. Electric Golden Pipe Organ has 27 black and white keys—plays 2 chromatic octaves in full bodied organ tone. Music book, electric cord included. (81373F) $20.00.

Automatic Player Drum *by Emenee*, beats a marching rhythm when handle is turned. Reinforced metal frame. Comes with 2 polished hardwood sticks for manual playing. Colorful American Eagle and Flag motif design around outside. (81373G) $4.00.

Spinet Piano and Bench *by Jaymor*. 30-key instrument with 2½ octaves, chromatically tuned. Blond finish on hardwood. 22 in. high, 20 in. wide, 13½ in. deep. (81373H) $26.98. Smaller 25-key Spinet and Bench in same finish. 18x17x11 in. deep. (81373H1) $14.98.

Encourage the urge to build with these Giant Building Bricks created *by National Games*. Set of 12 red bricks, each 12¼x16¼x3¼ in. made of durable fibre-board. In corrugated chest. (81373I) $6.98.

Doing dolly's laundry is fun with this steel Automatic Washer and Dryer *by Structo*. Little "Mothers" can care for dolls while machine washes, spin dries, shuts off automatically. Battery operated. (81373K) $6.98.

Hours of absorbing interest in this Venus Paradise Pencil Set. 8 pre-sketched drawings and 12 pencils (81373L) $2.00. Set with 15 pencils (81373L1) $2.50. 16 drawings, 24 pencils (81373L2) $5.00.

70G

RECAPTURING CHRISTMASES PAST

Nostalgia buffs will be delighted to know they can still revisit some of the things they remember from their childhood. Decorations, ornaments, toys, department store memorabilia, a taste of Hough Bakeries, and the Mr. Jingeling experience are among them.

MR. JINGELING TODAY

Mr. Jingeling is now a registered trademark of Traditions Alive Company. John Awarski of Traditions Alive says: "The big thing that people want is a replacement for their Mr. Jingeling key. They know they got one when they were a kid, but somehow it got torn, lost, disintegrated, or whatever. So we had an original key, took it to a printer and said, 'Duplicate it.' We are making them available, so people can capture that little bit of memory." For Mr. Jingeling merchandise and information, including live appearances by the present-day Mr. Jingeling, Jonathan Wilhelm, visit the website: www.mrjingeling.com.

TOYS FOR GIRLS, BOYS AND THEIR NOSTALGIA-LOVING PARENTS

At Big Fun, with locations in Cleveland Heights and on the west side of Cleveland, you can rediscover some of your favorite Christmas toys from the past. Playboy.com called it one of the coolest stores in America. Owner Steve Presser says: "People come into Big Fun to buy for themselves something they wanted as a child, or a toy that got lost, stolen, broken or sold by their mothers when they went off to college. To get a toy from your childhood means you're getting something that isn't being manufactured today."

VINTAGE DECORATIONS, WINDOW DISPLAYS AND DEPARTMENT STORE MEMORABILIA

Stop in at Flower Child to surround yourself with memories from yesteryear—see department store memorabilia and the seasonal Christmas display as well as clothes, furniture, and more. Expect to revisit things such as the Twigbee Bears and the red carpet from Higbee's. Owner Joe Valenti worked for Higbee's

Big Fun
1814 Coventry Rd.
Cleveland Heights
216-371-4386
www.bigfunbigfun.com

11512 Clifton Blvd.
Cleveland
216-631-4386
www.bigfunbigfun.com

Flower Child
11508 Clifton Blvd.
Cleveland
216-939-9933
www.flowerchildvintage.com

at one time, and says: "When Christmas would come, they would always run this big red runner up the center aisle. It used to get dirty in front of the door, and they would throw it away. I had an apartment back then and said I'd just save it and put it in my garage. I saved it for years, and when I opened the store, I did the same thing they did at Higbee's. I have a piece of the carpet—people come in to visit the carpet—and the original Higbee's boughs, the ones we hung in the store every year."

CHRISTMAS ORNAMENTS AND LOCAL CHRISTMAS MEMORABILIA

Hixson's in Lakewood not only sells some of the ornament designs used on White House trees, you'll also find a collection of local memorabilia. Remember the giant Raggedy Ann doll from *A Christmas Story*? She lives at Hixson's. Visit the year-round Timely Trims Christmas shop, including ornaments that have been used on White House Christmas trees and a selection of ornaments designed by Bill Hixson.

A HOUSE FOR MOVIE-LOVERS

Visit *A Christmas Story* House and Museum, open year-round, or visit the website and order a Leg Lamp. Owner Brian Jones says eighty-five percent of his business is online. However, there is plenty to recommend an in-person visit. "When people travel, they look for stuff that's off the beaten path. If they're coming to Cleveland, it's not your average tourist attraction. Our tour guides are all fans. The museum features behind-the-scenes photos and costumes. There are toys, and the chalkboard from the school."

A TASTE OF THE PAST

Started by Archie Garner, formerly the head baker at the catering department of Hough Bakeries, you can order some of the specialties you remember, such as cakes and petits fours at Archie's Lakeshore Bakery.

Hixson's, Inc.
14125 Detroit Ave.
Lakewood
216-521-9277
www.timelytrims.com

A Christmas Story House and Museum
3159 West 11th St.
Cleveland
216-298-4919
www.achristmasstoryhouse.com

Archie's Lakeshore Bakery
14906 Lake Shore Blvd.
Cleveland
216-481-4188

PHOTO CREDITS

p. 2, two on left, David C. Davis, courtesy of the Dave Davis Family; right, Rob Lucas, courtesy of Lake Metroparks

p. 3, left, Stephen Bellamy, courtesy of Candace Bohn; right, courtesy of the Cleveland Public Library

p. 4, courtesy of Shaker Heights Public Library Local History Collection

p. 5, courtesy of Shaker Heights Public Library Local History Collection

p. 6, CSU*

p. 7, top, Rob Lucas, courtesy of Joe Valenti, Flower Child; bottom, Stephen Bellamy, courtesy of Joe Valenti

p. 8, Top and bottom, Stephen Bellamy, courtesy of Joe Valenti, Flower Child; center, Stephen Bellamy, courtesy of the author

p. 9, top, CSU; bottom, courtesy of Bonnie Jacobson

p. 10, CSU

p. 11, Stephen Bellamy, courtesy of Lake Metroparks

p. 12, Stephen Bellamy, courtesy of Candace Bohn

p. 13, Rob Lucas, courtesy of Joe Valenti, Flower Child

p. 14, top left and top right, CSU; left center, courtesy of Lake Metroparks; bottom, Stephen Bellamy, courtesy of Candace Bohn

p. 15, bottom left, CSU; top right, Stephen Bellamy, courtesy of the author, center and bottom, Stephen Bellamy and Rob Lucas, courtesy of Lake Metroparks

p. 16, CSU

p. 17, left, Stephen Bellamy, courtesy of Candace Bohn; Rob Lucas, courtesy of Joe Valenti, Flower Child

p. 18, Stephen Bellamy, courtesy of Candace Bohn

p. 19, top right, Stephen Bellamy, courtesy of Candace Bohn; bottom left, CSU, bottom right, courtesy of Lake Metroparks

p. 20, left, top right, and lower right, CSU; lower left, courtesy of Lake Metroparks

p. 21, bottom left, CSU; center, courtesy of Lake Metroparks; top right, Stephen Bellamy, courtesy of Candace Bohn

p. 22, CSU

p. 23, left, CSU; right, Rob Lucas, courtesy of Joe Valenti, Flower Child

p. 24, top, Stephen Bellamy, courtesy of Candace Bohn; bottom, CSU

p. 25, courtesy of Cleveland Play House

p. 26, courtesy of the author

p. 27, left, John Gerbetz, courtesy of Dennis Nahat; right, author's collection

p. 28, top, CSU; bottom, John Gerbetz, courtesy of Dennis Nahat

p. 31, courtesy of John Gorman

p. 32, top, Stephen Bellamy, courtesy of the author; bottom, photograph by A.R. Thiel, courtesy of the Archives of the Musical Arts Association

p. 33, courtesy of the Archives of the Musical Arts Association

p. 34, courtesy of the National Cleveland-Style Polka Hall of Fame and Museum

p. 35, Stephen Bellamy, courtesy of Pat Fernberg

p. 36, top, Stephen Bellamy; bottom, courtesy of A Christmas Story House & Museum

p. 37, courtesy of the author

p. 38, courtesy of A Chrismas Story House & Museum

p. 39, GE'S Nela Park

p. 40, GE'S Nela Park

p. 41, CSU

p. 42, CSU

p. 43, CSU

p. 44, courtesy of Richard Konisiewicz

p. 45, left, CSU; courtesy of Stephen Bellamy

p. 46, George Ghetia

p. 48, author's collection

p. 49, courtesy of Pat Fernberg

p. 50, author's collection

p. 51, Perry Cragg, courtesy of John Stark Bellamy II

p. 52, George Ghetia, courtesy of the author

p. 53, Richard Gray

p. 55, courtesy of a private collector

p. 56, courtesy of the R.J. King Family

p. 57, George Ghetia

p. 59, courtesy of Pat Fernberg

p. 60, top, courtesy of Pat Fernberg; bottom, CSU

p. 61, Stephen Bellamy, courtesy of Marilou Suszko

p. 62, Gary Cardot Photography

p. 63, CSU

p. 64, top, Stephen Bellamy; bottom, Rob Lucas, courtesy of Bill Hixson, Hixson's Flower Barn

p. 65, top, CSU; right, W.P. Nebel, courtesy of Hope Lutheran Church; bottom, Stephen Bellamy, courtesy of a Private Collector

p. 66, left, Rob Lucas, courtesy of Bill Hixson, Hixson's Flower Barn; right, CSU

p. 67, Stephen Bellamy

p. 68, Stephen Bellamy

p. 69, top left, White House photo, courtesy of Bill Hixson; top right and bottom, Rob Lucas and Stephen Bellamy, courtesy of Bill Hixson, Hixson's Flower Barn

p. 70, top, Rob Lucas, courtesy of Bill Hixson, Hixson's Flower Barn; bottom, courtesy of the author

p. 71, Stephen Bellamy, courtesy of Joe Valenti, Flower Child

p. 72, Stephen Bellamy, courtesy of Candace Bohn; bottom, Stephen Bellamy

p. 73, top, CSU; bottom, Stephen Bellamy

p. 74, CSU

p. 75, Stephen Bellamy

p. 79, Stephen Bellamy, courtesy of Candace Bohn

p. 80, CSU

p. 81, courtesy of The Macias Family

p. 82, courtesy of Stephen Bellamy

p. 83, Stephen Bellamy, courtesy of a Private Collector

p. 84, courtesy of The Macias Family

p. 85, top, David C. Davis, courtesy of the Dave Davis Family; bottom, courtesy of The Macias Family

p. 86, CSU

p. 87, Rob Lucas, courtesy of Joe Valenti, Flower Child

p. 88, top, CSU; bottom, Rob Lucas, courtesy of Joe Valenti, Flower Child

p. 89, top, Stephen Bellamy, courtesy of Candace Bohn; bottom, CSU

p. 90, CSU

p. 91, Jonathan Wayne, toys courtesy of Steve Presser, Big Fun

p. 92, courtesy of the Jack Harrison Family

p. 93, left, Hastings & Willinger, courtesy of the Archives of the Musical Arts Association; right, courtesy of Bunny Breslin

p. 94, CSU

p. 95, left, author's collection; right, courtesy of Candace Bohn

p. 96, left, Jonathan Wayne, toys courtesy of Steve Presser, Big Fun, right, Rob Lucas; bottom, Stephen Bellamy, courtesy of Candace Bohn

p. 97, CSU

p. 98, CSU

p. 99, key collection courtesy of Ron Newell, author's collection; left, Stephen Bellamy, courtesy of Lake Metroparks

p. 100, CSU

p. 101, Stephen Bellamy, courtesy of Joe Valenti, Flower Child

p. 102, courtesy of Lake Metroparks

p. 103, Rob Lucas, courtesy of Lake Metroparks

p. 104, left, Stephen Bellamy, courtesy of Lake Metroparks; right courtesy of Bob Burford

p. 105, Rob Lucas, courtesy of Lake Metroparks

p. 106, top, CSU; bottom, courtesy of the Cleveland Public Library

p. 107, left, courtesy of Ron Newell; right, CSU

p. 108, Jonathan Wayne, toys courtesy of Steve Presser, Big Fun

p. 109, left, Jonathan Wayne, toys courtesy of Steve Presser, Big Fun; right, Stephen Bellamy

p. 110, Jonathan Wayne, toys courtesy of Steve Presser, Big Fun

p. 111, top right, Stephen Bellamy; center right and bottom, Jonathan Wayne, toys courtesy of Steve Presser, Big Fun

p. 112, Jonathan Wayne, toys courtesy of Steve Presser, Big Fun

p. 113–115, Jonathan Wayne, toys courtesy of Steve Presser, Big Fun

p. 116, Stephen Bellamy, courtesy of a private collector

p. 117, Jonathan Wayne, toys courtesy of Steve Presser, Big Fun

p. 118, left Jonathan Wayne, courtesy of Stephen Bellamy; right, Jonathan Wayne, toys courtesy of Steve Presser, Big Fun

p. 119, top, CSU; bottom, courtesy of Jim Nolan; right, Stephen Bellamy, courtesy of Candace Bohn

p. 120, top, Stephen Bellamy, courtesy of Candace Bohn; bottom, Rob Lucas, courtesy of Lake Metroparks

p. 121, courtesy of Lake Metroparks

* CSU – Cleveland Press Collection, Cleveland State University

ACKNOWLEDGEMENTS

I am grateful to my husband Stephen Bellamy for the countless hours he has spent recording, photographing, interviewing, researching, and transcribing. This book would not have been possible without his talent and diligence.

I am indebted to Rob Lucas for the photography, research, and creative energy he contributed to this book.

The following individuals, institutions, and businesses have made Cleveland Christmas memories come to life by providing leads and photography, and by sharing their expertise and enthusiasm. In sharing their memories and knowledge, they have enriched us all and I thank them:

Lake Metroparks—Penitentiary Glen Reservation Nature Center manager Dan Burnett and exhibit naturalist Wendy Pittinger provided Halle's memorabilia; Ron Newell; Mary Krohmer, Director of Community Relations, Lake View Cemetery; Rev. Donald King, Pastor of Hope Lutheran Church; David Schuellerman, G.E.—Appliances and Lighting, Public Relations Program Manager, Nela Park; Beth Schreibman Gehring; Corey Atkins, Artistic Associate—Engagement, The Cleveland Play House; Barbara S. Robinson; Linda Jackson, Assistant Director of Community Engagement and Education, PlayhouseSquare; Dennis Nahat; Eleanor Blackman, Scholarly Resources & Special Collections, Kelvin Smith Library, CWRU; Jill Tatem, University Archivist, Case Western Reserve Univesity; The Archives of the Musical Arts Association and Deborah M. Hefling, Archivist; Larry Fox, Manager of the Cleveland Orchestra Store and Blossom Bandwagon Store; John Awarski, Traditions Alive; Joseph Valenti of Flower Child; Laurie Kincer, Readers' Advisory Specialist of Cuyahoga County Public Library; Mary Schreiber, Youth Collection Development Specialist, Cuyahoga County Public Library; Bill Hixson of Hixson's, Inc.; Steve Presser, Big Fun; April Miller, Communications Manager, Trinity Cathedral; Cindy Wyszynski, Boar's Head Festival Committee Chair; Brian Jones of A Christmas Story House & Museum; Ron Antonucci, Cleveland Public Library; Joe Valencic of the National Cleveland-Style Polka Hall of Fame and Museum; Richard Konisiewicz; Gary Cardot of Gary Cardot Photography; William P. Nebel; Glen Nekvasil; Ann Lee; Bonnie Jacobson; Sr. Donna Capuano, OSU; Bunny Breslin; Bob Burford; Steve Horniak; Casey Daniels; Pat Harrison and the Jack Harrison Family; Ellen Dunlay; Don Kissel and the Betty Kissel family; John Gorman; John Stark Bellamy II; Bob Tayek; Candace Bohn; Pat Fernberg; Laurie Orr; Lynette Macias; Bill Davis; Dave Davis; Pat Flynn; Jim Nolan; Richard Gray; Jill Froula; Denise Small; John Parratt; Mike Sanson; Dennis Gaughan; and Marilou Suszko. Also, no nostalgia book is complete without the memory-sharers, and I have been blessed with many in this project.

In addition to those already listed, I thank the following for their good memories and their generosity of spirit: Deanna Adams; Christopher G. Axelrod; Kathie Brown; Reginald Carter; Kathleen Cerveny; Katie Daley; Michael Angelo DiLauro; Tommy Fello; Diane Vogel Ferri; Janice Fleming Ghetia Orr; George Ghetia; Mary Ghetia; Jim Gelarden; Dickie Gildenmeister; Richard Gould; Debbie Jancsurak; Joe Jancsurak; The King Family: Tom King, Tim King, Ronnie King Whalen, Gerry King, Peggy King-Neumann, Dennis King, Brian King, Kevin King, Noreen King Hone, Rhea King Wightman, David King; Josephine Kovach; Bob Krummert; Nicole Loughman; Carol Lally; Lynne McLaughlin; Virginia Meil; Larry Morrow; Paul Negulescu; Erin O'Brien; Estelle Painter; Tom Papadimoulis; Nancy Reese; Marie Sandru; William Small; Katie Smith; Chris Spano; Jon Thibo; Bunny Sullivan Trepal; Cindy Washabaugh; and Helen Wirt.

And finally, in memoriam: Arlene M. Sterba passed away on August 25, 2012, a few weeks after sharing her Christmas memories for this book, with much laughter, sentiment and joy.

More Cleveland Memories...

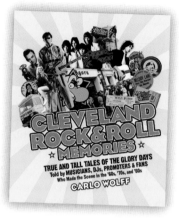

Cleveland Food Memories
by Gail Ghetia Bellamy

Remember when food was local? Cleveland companies made it, and local people sold it and ran the restaurants where we ate it. Now, take a delicious trip into the past.

Food makes powerful memories. Mention Hough Bakery and see how quickly we Clevelanders start to drool over just the thought of those long-lost white cakes. This book collects the fondest memories of Clevelanders who still ache for treats from the past. There were Frostees in the Higbee's basement. Popcorn balls at Euclid Beach. Burgers at Manner's or Mawby's. Entertainment-filled nights at Alpine Village. Mustard at old Municipal Stadium . . . and so much more.

Richly illustrated.

Paperback / 112 pages / 209 photos

Cleveland Rock & Roll Memories
by Carlo Wolff

Music fans who grew up with Rock & Roll in Cleveland remember a golden age. We were young, so was the music, and the sense of freedom and excitement the Rock and Roll scene delivered was electric. This book collects the favorite memories of Clevelanders who made that scene: fans, musicians, DJs, reporters, club owners, and more.

There were great clubs, like the Agora, where every big band seemed to break in the 1970s. Trendsetting radio stations, from A.M.'s WIXY 1260 to F.M.'s groundbreaking "Home of the Buzzard", WMMS. And all those memorable shows. The free Coffee Break Concerts—remember Springsteen just when he hit it big? The gigantic World Series of Rock. Nights on the lawn at Blossom (including local favorites the Michael Stanley Band and their record-setting sellout streak).

Paperback / 136 pages / 203 photos

Cleveland Amusement Park Memories
by David and Diane Francis

Northeast Ohioans who grew up visiting amusement parks in the 1940s through 1970s will cherish the memories captured in this book, which includes Euclid Beach Park, Luna Park, Geauga Lake Park, Puritas Springs Park, White City, Memphis Kiddie Park, Geneva-on-the-Lake, and others.

Each boisterous, colorful, exciting park had its own personality, its own alluring smells and sounds. At Euclid Beach it was the stately sycamores and the unforgettable odor of the lake and of damp earth beneath the pier. At Puritas Springs, the odor of warm oil on the chain of the Cyclone coaster. The chatter of Monkey Island at Luna Park, the sharp reports of the Shooting Gallery at Geauga Lake.

Draws on the authors' own extensive archive and on the memories of fellow park buffs to create a vivid, nostalgic portrait of days gone by.

Paperback / 128 pages / 192 photos

More information and samples at:
www.grayco.com